"Boyung Lee accomplishes something the field of religious education has needed for a long time—a deep engagement with the classic work of Maria Harris through the lens of postcolonial biblical and theological studies. This book is written with a deft touch for and awareness of the needs of mainline church educators, while at the same time drawing on the best of recent scholarship. What can and should a word like 'community' mean when we live in a richly complex and diverse world of many cultures? Further, how do we invite the insights of biblical communities through time into our discernment and learning? Dr. Lee offers exciting answers to these questions and interweaves them with pragmatic tools for living into beloved community. This book will be a required text in my religious education classes."
—MARY HESS, Professor of Educational Leadership, Luther Seminary

"Basing her advocacy for a communal faith formation and ministry on the origin of ancient Israel as 'the people of God' and a critical assessment of the popular image of the church as the body of Christ in addition to her own deep insights into other-than-Euro concepts of community and the tension between communalism and individualism, Boyung Lee proposes employing a pedagogy for 'liberating interdependence' that moves from a still divisive multiculturality to an inclusive interculturality for a more just future. Drawing on solid progressive understandings of twentieth-century Christian education theorists such as Thomas Groome and Maria Harris, Lee invites and challenges the seminary and church teacher/preacher to emulate her own embodied pedagogic practice that comes alive through firsthand accounts of sensitive pastoral contextual analysis as well as adult-learning-based teaching-learning, culminating in two extremely helpful—and hopeful—examples of teaching the Bible using postcolonial biblical interpretation. An indispensable resource for all who long for a workable approach to education and faith formation in struggling mainline Christian communities of faith."
—GREER ANNE WENH-IN NG, Professor Emerita, Emmanuel College, Victoria University in the University of Toronto

"*Transforming Congregations through Community* extends the conversation in the field of Christian religious education. Dr. Boyung Lee offers us an expanded vision of a community of faith approach to Christian education. Combining biblical research with postcolonial theology and intercultural education, she challenges approaches to community that merely seek to build a home for those familiar with each other. We are challenged to embody a community that makes a difference, that connects us in solidarity across cultural boundaries, and that reaches out in love to the world we share. Through concrete exercises, we are guided to make this vision a reality in the ministries of congregations. Dr. Lee's vision thus can become a reality for churches living faith and hope."
– JACK L. SEYMOUR, Professor of Religious Education, Garrett-Evangelical Theological Seminary, and editor of *Religious Education*

Transforming Congregations through Community

Faith Formation from the Seminary to the Church

BOYUNG LEE

WESTMINSTER
JOHN KNOX PRESS
LOUISVILLE · KENTUCKY

First edition
Published by Westminster John Knox Press
Louisville, Kentucky

14 15 16 17 18 19 20 21 22—10 9 8 7 6 5 4 3 2

Chapter 10 is an updated version of an article that originally appeared as Boyung Lee, "Toward Liberating Interdependence: Exploring an Intercultural Pedagogy," *Religious Education* 105, no. 3 (Summer 2010): 283-98; reprinted with the permission of Taylor and Francis Group.

All Scripture quotations are from New Revised Standard Version Bible, copyright © 1989 National Council of the Churches of Christ in the United States of America. Used by permission.

Book design by Sharon Adams
Cover design by Dilu Nicholas

Library of Congress Cataloging-in-Publication Data
Lee, Boyung.
  Transforming congregations through community : faith formation from the seminary to the church / Boyung Lee. -- First edition.
      pages cm
  Includes bibliographical references and index.
  ISBN 978-0-664-23330-3 (alk. paper)
  1. Communities--Religious aspects--Christianity. 2. Faith development. 3. Spiritual formation. I. Title.
  BV625.L44 2013
  253--dc23

                          2013031725

∞ The paper used in this publication meets the minimum requirements of the American National Standard for Information Sciences—Permanence of Paper for Printed Library Materials, ANSI Z39.48-1992.

Most Westminster John Knox Press books are available at special quantity discounts when purchased in bulk by corporations, organizations, and special-interest groups. For more information, please e-mail SpecialSales@wjkbooks.com.

To My beloved husband,
The Rev. Landon Tracy Archer Summers, Ed.D., J.D. (1959–2011)

Contents

of curriculum, which is different from the narrowly understood conventional view, and show a holistic view of curriculum to help mainline churches move towards communal ways of being the church.

Both of these principles are well articulated by religious educator Maria Harris in her book *Fashion Me a People: Curriculum in the Church.*[1] Most of my students at the Graduate Theological Union are very excited about her proposals to move the church towards being a transformative community. However, others express their frustration at not being able to translate the principles for their own particular ministerial contexts. Therefore, in Chapter 6 I address those concerns raised by my students and provide a step-by-step guideline for developing a curriculum for communal faith formation.

In Part 3, I present detailed educational methodologies and examples for communal faith formation. Particularly, I show what "the entire life of the church" as a curriculum would look like. In Chapter 7, I propose a communal preaching and Bible study model and method that utilize postcolonial biblical hermeneutics, which conjoins critical thinking with multiethnic, multireligious, and multicultural voices. Through this model I challenge mainline Christians to reconsider their notions about community and to redraw the boundaries for God's reign. In Chapter 8, I continue to explore a new way to teach the Bible. Here, I introduce the Traveling Bible Study to provide people who experience learning cul-de-sacs in church education programs to get easier access to faith formation. This study model is also designed to help people apply theology to places beyond the church; to cultivate meaningful connections between their study and daily life contexts; and, thus, to expand the boundaries of community. In Chapter 9, I focus on the church's administrative system. To create and promote a sense of community, both programs and the administrative structure of the church should be communal. However, many faith communities only focus on communal programs with a compartmentalized structure which, in fact, contradicts their efforts. In this chapter I explore processes to create a communal administrative system that can strengthen the sense of community. In the last chapter, as an alternative to the current prevailing multiculturalism of mainline churches, an individualistic and colonial way of engaging with different racial and ethnic communities, I offer interculturalism and explore how it helps the mainline church to build a communal church that is also an interculturally engaging church. Throughout the book, I conclude each chapter with discussion topics and praxis exercises. My hope is that this are as serious as those of individualism: e.g., social harmony at the cost of the powerless and the deprivation of each member's individuality. Therefore in this book, I advocate a model of community that achieves a dual task: first, acknowledgment that a communal worldview respects human groups' relatedness; and second, overcoming notions of community that would sacrifice one's sacred calling as an individual to social hierarchy and nepotism.

I find such an ideal community in the Hebrew Bible and the Christian Scripture. In Chapters 2 and 3, I examine biblical notions of community as reflected in the People of God and the Body of Christ. Interpreting from a postcolonial feminist perspective, I find that biblical community offers a much-needed, albeit problematic, sense of community for the mainline church and theological education as it simultaneously uplifts humanity's communal nature and each member's unique individuality and accountability. Although a biblical sense of community provides fundamental directions for this book, the highlight of the book is Part 2 where I explore pedagogical principles to transform current mainline churches to such a community in the twenty-first century.

In Part 2, I argue that if the mainline rethinks its ministry through pedagogical reformation, a healthy community can be created and promoted. I introduce and utilize particular foundational educational principles that are very familiar to religious educators but not necessarily to ministers and theologians. The first principle is that schooling and education are not the same. Although schooling is a form of education, many people misunderstand it as an equal concept to education. Schooling mainly happens in classroom contexts with teachers who have authority to transmit knowledge to students who are recipients of deposited information, whereas education is a holistic endeavor that involves people's whole being and their entire community. It happens in every life context of the people, including schools. In Chapter 4, I show concrete differences between the two and argue that the mainline can create a healthy community by approaching its entire ministry as an educational endeavor.

The second principle is that education in the church happens in and through everything we do beyond the explicit educational programming. Therefore, a church's entire ministry of worship, fellowship, teaching, mission, and proclamation can serve as its curriculum. Even without participating in an educational event, people teach and learn how to be a member of the community through the church's basic forms of ministry. In Chapter 5, through several concrete examples, I explain the meaning

Preface

This book is not about church growth or revitalization. Rather it explores ways to transform individualism in theological education and ministry and presents a pedagogical model for communal faith and ministry. Notwithstanding that, the revitalization of the mainline has been on my mind throughout the time that I have worked on this manuscript. As the global recession has worsened since 2008, its impact is reshaping mainline churches and theological schools as reflected in their shaky financial stability and shrinking enrollment. Churches and seminaries are trying to come up with solutions for this unfamiliar phenomenon by reinventing their identity, mission, and modes of curriculum delivery. Both clergy and laity and theological educators and students alike constantly ask hard questions: Will the mainline church survive in the twenty-first century? How do we stop the mainline from declining? Will theological education, as it is, make sense to the twenty-first-century church? What should we do differently to be relevant for the changing time? The hardest part of finding answers to these questions is that no one seems to have clear answers, and the future is so uncertain.

Much to the disappointment of readers, I also do not have answers to these questions. Rather, in this book, I offer a Christian religious educator's analysis of the current situation of the mainline church and make pedagogical suggestions for its transformation. If most of us are uncertain about the future of the church and theological education, I believe that it is necessary for us to closely look at what is working, or not working, in our current ministry and education and find clues for the future. Integrating my own experiences in pastoral ministry and theological education over the last twenty-five years, I offer analyses and suggestions for the mainline and its theological education from an Asian American postcolonial feminist religious educator's perspective.

In this book I particularly explore ways to transform individualism, which I consider as the fundamental problem in our society as well as in theological education and ministry of the mainline, and present a pedagogical model for communal faith and ministry. There have been numerous critiques of individualism in theological discourse, and diverse small-group ministry models have been introduced to the local church; yet individualism is still a prevailing feature of the mainline churches. Throughout my personal and scholarly engagements, I have found that small-group movements, which are supposed to create and promote community, have actually perpetuated individualism in the mainline. As someone who grew up in Korea, one of the most communal cultures that still upholds almost a pure form of Confucian communal values, I have often found that my definition of community is not necessarily the same as that of my colleagues and friends who grew up in the United States. However, I could not explain the difference until one of my mentors, the late Christian educator Dr. David Ng, helped me to articulate it during a dinner conversation at the 1996 annual meeting of American Academy of Religion in New Orleans. The East Asian notion of community is based on solidarity, whereas the mainline US idea of community is more associated with relationships. A community of solidarity arising from common responsibilities and interests of its members cannot be easily broken, even when members are not satisfied with the community. However, if members understand community as relationships, then individual needs often have higher priority than those of the community. The members can relatively easily cut themselves off from relationships when and if they feel the community does not serve their needs.

In this book, I first analyze how individualistic the mainline's views of community are through a comparison with those of communal cultures (Chapter 1). I call the mainline's notion of community "collectivism" and that of communal cultures like East Asian countries "communalism." However, I do not offer a communal culture's model as an alternative to the mainline. Although communal cultures acknowledge and uphold the fundamental nature of the human as a communal being, they have their own problems, which in my opinion

PART 1

UNDERSTANDING COMMUNITY AND A BIBLICAL CALL FOR COMMUNAL FAITH

Chapter 1

Individualism, Collectivism, and Communalism

What Do We Mean by Community?

"Is this *OUR* husband?" "I am so glad to meet you, *OUR* husband!" These were words used by some of my students when they meet my late husband. To introduce communal cultures' view of community and compare it with that of many North Americans, I often frame my class discussions using Korean communal linguistics. Although Koreans have words for "I," "me," "my," and "mine," we seldom use them. For example, the most culturally acceptable way to introduce one's spouse is by saying, "This is *OUR* husband," or "This is *OUR* wife." Although "my husband" is grammatically correct, using "I" language is culturally awkward.

Korean communal linguistics originated in a communal worldview. Koreans, like many African, Hispanic, Native, and other Asian American cultures, view the person as a part of a whole. In contrast, most

European American cultures see the person as an independent and autonomous entity. These differences in the view of the person are reflected in each worldview's concept of community. In communal cultures, community is generally identified with people's solidarity, regardless of their individual circumstances. In individually oriented worldviews, the community is constituted of individuals who share similar interests.[1] For example, a Korean word for "group," *moim*, originated from the word *mom*, "body." Thus "group" in Korean means people *within* the same boundary; those who identify themselves as one body. Conceptually, this is very different from its English counterpart, which connotes a relationship between their units instead of organic wholeness.

In this chapter, I compare concepts of community. By focusing on different notions of the person, I invite readers to identify the concept of community used in their faith communities. Throughout, I frame this discussion with observations by social scientists, especially their research on anthropology; namely, I ask what it means to be an individual, and, more importantly, what identity an individual has relative to others, and whether "others" connotes a group in the Korean linguistic sense or *many* individuals.

SMALL AS BIG

For religious institutions, small groups are the rage. According to Robert Wuthnow, who studied small groups in American religious settings in partnership with the Gallup organization, about 40 percent of adult Americans are currently involved in some form of small group, and approximately 60 percent of these members belong to a group formally associated with a church or synagogue.[2] In other words, almost half of adult Americans across racial, gender, age, class, and geographic lines regularly participate in small groups. Although the number of mainline Christians involved in small groups is not as big as that of conservative Protestant Christians,[3] small groups are a growing phenomenon in the mainline church. Cell groups, home groups, covenant groups, ChristCare groups, in addition to Bible studies, which constitute the most widespread small group, cut a noteworthy swath across the mainline.

Regarding this phenomenon, Wuthnow observes that small groups

Their ambitions for me have come true, and I am honored to be their daughter. And a thankful huzzah to my two adorable stepchildren, Clara Elaine and Landon Jack, who have brought me tremendous joy as a parent! I am so grateful to be Oma to these two incredible young communal persons. The love and support of Sharon and Ron Lewkowitz taught me that friendship across religious, cultural, and ethnic boundaries can be thicker than family ties. They embody the "kindom" of God on earth, and I am so blessed to be a part of the kinship. Finally, THANK YOU to my loving husband, Landon Tracy Archer Summers, who figuratively—but it sometimes seems literally—broke his own life into pieces to help me realize my dreams. As a Methodist minister, an educator, a linguist, and a lawyer, he provided not only spousal support while I was working on this project but also critical feedback to the earlier version of the book. Although our time together was too short, I know in my heart that our marriage was perfect because of his patience and love. To him I dedicate this book.

practical theology book helps seminary students, clergy, and laity of progressive mainline denominations to explore ways to revitalize the church through transforming individualism in theological education and diverse ministry contexts.

There are many people who shared in the process of creating this project and who have been an important part of my journey as a communitarian theologian and educator. To all of them I would like to express my indescribable thanks. First, I would like to thank my parishioners in Korea, California, and New England, especially those whom I met in Sinbanpo Methodist Church, and Dr. Kejoon Lee, and those at Bolton United Methodist Church in Bolton, Connecticut. Without their generosity and support, this project might still be germinating. I also would like to acknowledge the special friendship offered to me by some of my friends, especially during the difficult time I experienced after the sudden death of my spouse: Jinwon Kim, Rev. Kristin Langstraat, Dansil Kye, Rev. KyungmoonYoon, Dr. Elizabeth Conde-Frazier, Dr. Soo Young Kwon of Yonsei University, and my childhood friends Eunjoo and Meehyun. I am ever grateful to have them as my friends. Through their friendship, I have experienced the healing power of a community of friends.

I am also in great debt to my esteemed colleagues at Pacific School of Religion (PSR) in Berkeley, California, who genuinely care about creating a just community. I am proud to be their colleague. Judith Berling, Jeffrey Kuan, Benny Liew, Fumitaka Matsuoka, and Randi Walker, along with their families, created a true family-like community for me when I thought that I had lost one. My friends and mentors from Pacific, Asian, North American Asian Women in Theology and Ministry (PANAAWTM), especially Seung Ai Yang, Rita Brock, Kwok Pui Lan, Anne Joh, and Nami Kim, helped me to believe that a just academic community is also possible and exists in real life. A special thanks also goes to my students at PSR and the Graduate Theological Union (GTU) who are ever eager to ask critical questions and challenge my assumptions. They comprise part of my philosophical checks and balances. Among them I give special thanks to Beth Ritter-Conn and A. Vanessa Hawkins, doctoral students at the GTU, who read the entire manuscript, providing careful editing support. Without their help, this book would not have been the same.

I give very special thanks to my family whose godly love I cannot find words to describe, especially to Mom and Dad, who have taken my ministry and scholarship to heart with sacrifice, prayer, and love.

provide a sense of community and family in the midst of "turbulent upheaval." According to Wuthnow, the average family moves at least once every three years, and half of those families are restructured by divorce.[4] Lonely Americans find support and encouragement for life in small groups as they care for each other, pray with one another, and share stories of life together. The American church's increasing attention to small-group ministries may be a response to an apprehended yearning for community by its constituency. It also may be an effort by churches to calm angst about changes in the social order. Sadly, though, the traditional ministry of the church, which greatly depends on clergy leadership for spiritual growth, arguably is inefficient and inadequate to respond to these changes. Weekend services are no longer convenient for many Americans because of members' demanding careers and family lives, so both conservative and mainline churches find small groups to be efficient alternative ministries. Small groups waylay the cost of physical plants and are attractive to those looking for support groups, ones that sometimes make few demands.[5]

Based on Wuthnow's observations, one could argue that the popular notion of Americans as alienated individualists is no longer valid: that Americans are becoming communalists like those in other parts of the world. However, if one looks closely at the nature of small groups, one easily sees that small groups typically exhibit what I call "collectivism," rather than communalism. The sense of community undergirding the current American trend in small groups is far different from that of communalists for they lack solidarity and kinship-like relationships; rather, the notion of community in mainline small groups is more like a gathering of individuals in reciprocal relationships. These groups are made up of individuals who share similar needs and interests. Individuals purportedly gather on a regular basis to develop their personal spirituality. Members support and pray for each other, especially for those who are in crisis. They even make occasional sacrifices for other group members. However, if they find the group burdensome or unfulfilling, they frequently abandon it.[6] Wuthnow's observation about group identity is directly on point:

> Members are not people who are disproportionately oriented toward community or toward fitting in, helping others, or bending their interests toward the will of the group. They are strong individualists who bring their individual needs and interests to their group.[7]

Hereto, group identity is predicated on personal attainment, which rarely entails sacrifice. I will present my own research findings shortly, ones that parallel Wuthnow's observations. In the interim, I turn to a discussion about how individualism and communalism view the world and community differently.

THE TWO DIFFERENT VIEWS OF THE PERSON: INDIVIDUALISM AND COMMUNALISM

The topic of individualism and communalism was a major research subject in Geert Hofstede's *Culture's Consequences*.[8] After analyzing about 117,000 protocols that IBM collected from its own employees in 66 countries, Hofstede defines individualism and communalism as follows:

> Individualism pertains to societies in which the ties between individuals are loose: everyone is expected to look after himself or herself and his or her immediate family. Collectivism as its opposite pertains to societies in which people from birth onwards are integrated into strong, cohesive ingroups, which throughout people's lifetime continue to protect them in exchange for unquestioning loyalty.[9]

Individualism and communalism are two completely different cultural patterns that lead people to view the world and life through different lenses. Harry Triandis, who has done extensive studies on the two patterns of culture, articulates the differences on the basis of ingroup/outgroup dynamics.[10] In communal societies, emphasis is on:

a) the views, needs, and goals of the ingroup rather than those of oneself;

b) social norms and duty defined by the ingroup rather than by one's pleasure;

c) beliefs shared with the ingroup rather than on beliefs that distinguish oneself from the ingroup; and

d) great readiness to cooperate with ingroup members.

Individualistic societies emphasize:

a) one's own views, needs, and goals rather than those of others;

b) pleasure, fun, personal enjoyment rather than social norms
or duty as defined by others;

c) one's beliefs as unique; and

d) maximizing one's own outcomes.

In general, the individualistic cultural pattern is found in most northern
and western regions of Europe and in North America, whereas
the communal cultural pattern is prevalent in Asia, Africa, Latin America,
and the Pacific.[11] These cultural differences result in different emphases
on relationship and behavior patterns. Individualistic societies emphasize
"I" consciousness: emotional independence, individual initiative, right to
privacy, and specific friendship. Separated from family, religion, and
agreement as sources of authority, duty, and moral example,
individualists seek to work out their own form of action by
autonomously pursuing happiness and satisfying their wants. Unlike
individualistic societies, communal societies stress "we" consciousness:
communal identity, emotional dependence, group-minded friendship,
group decision making, and particularism.[12] A person in communal
cultures is perceived as an adjunct of the family system, and the identity
of an individual is neither independent nor important. Group cohesion
and conformity dominate the family structure. Therefore the needs and
goals of people are often sacrificed for the attainment of the community's interests. C. Harry Hui and Harry Trandis sum up these
characteristics of communalism as "Concern of Others."[13]

COMMUNAL CONCEPT OF THE PERSON

Communalists view themselves primarily as parts of the whole, as clearly
reflected in the Chinese word for person, a notion shared by most East
Asians. The word for person in Chinese (人) connotes two people
leaning against each other. The pictographic syntax of the word assumes
sharing of ego boundaries, and, accordingly, the formation of
personhood is in relationship with that of others. The communalists'
notion of person includes the attributes of the group to which a person
belongs, whether that group is that of a larger region or of a tribe. For
example, whenever unacquainted Koreans meet, it is very common for
them immediately to determine their possible relatedness by asking
which region they are from, which schools they attended, and to which
surname family branch they belong. For instance, if two people belong

to the same branch of the Lee family, the next step is to determine their respective generation by determining one another's own or parents' and grandparents' shared generation names. This way a younger generation can show proper respect to older members of his or her family. As soon as Koreans determine their relatedness, the two immediately revere this "we" relationship. Once relationships are established, communalists are expected to accede to the goals of the group rather than to esteem personal goals. One is expected to do what the group expects, asks, or demands, without undermining it or voicing opposition.[14]

When conflict exists between the group and the individual, communalists are expected to choose the goals of the group for the sake of its harmony, even sacrificing their personal lives. Since a communalist's personhood is only defined in relationship with that of others, it is important for communalists to maintain good relationships with ingroup members, even if from a self-serving perspective it is not in their best interests to do so. As long as communalists consistently show loyalty to the group, the group will ensure support and security for each person.

Another example of the communalist worldview is seen in Korean and Japanese linguistics. As mentioned earlier, Koreans use "we" or "our" even when they refer to their own thing: "our house" or "our husband" instead of "my house" or "my husband." Korean cultural convention expects a married woman, who neither shares her husband with others nor has an intention to do so, to say "our husband" even though "my husband" is grammatically correct. Here, *We* does not mean the coexistence of *I* and *You* as independent individual units; rather it indicates that, for example, *You* and *You* and *You* and *I* are the same reality. As Soo-Won Lee observe, "I and you exist not as separate units but as a unified one. At the moment when two individuals abandon their own perspective and put themselves in their partner's shoes, they become one, not a separate two."[15]

A similar example is found in Japanese linguistics. The English word "self" is usually translated by the Japanese word *jibun*, and vice versa. However, unlike the English word for self, *jibun* connotes "one's share of the shared life space";[16] that is, oneself as an inseparable part of ourselves. So when two Japanese people exchange greetings by asking how the other party is, the customary way of saying it is, "How is *jibun*?" which literally means, "How is ourselves?"[17]

In sum, persons in communal societies can be fully understood only in connection with the larger social whole. "Others are included within the boundaries of the self."[18] Accordingly, attachments, relatedness, connectedness, oneness, and dependency among people are much more important than independence and individuality in communal society. Communalists find themselves adrift when they fail to adjust to the community to which they belong. Since everyone needs one another, this need forces people to be vulnerable when facing the loss of the relationship.

INDIVIDUALISTIC VIEW OF THE PERSON

A "healthy" adult in the individualistic culture is described as an autonomous, competitive, independent, achievement- and freedom-oriented individual.[19] Accordingly, autonomy, separation, and independence are emphasized as positive characteristics. Development means moving toward independence. Maturity is understood as self-reliance and personal autonomy. Mature and healthy people are expected to be in charge of themselves and in control of their own behavior. Robert Bellah, who has done extensive studies on American individualism, gives an example of this individualistic value and way of life. Brian, one of his interviewees says:

> The rule of thumb out here is that if you've got the money, honey, you can do things as long as your thing doesn't destroy someone else's property, or interrupt their sleep, or bother their privacy, then that's fine. If you want to go in your house and smoke marijuana and shoot dope and get all screwed up, that's your business, but don't bring that out on the street, don't expose my children to it, just do your thing.[20]

Thus, individualists are motivated by their own preferences, needs, and rights.[21] If an individual has personal goals that are inconsistent with the goals of his or her groups, it is regarded as natural that the individual attempts to reach his or her goals and ignore those of the group. In other words, an individual is the only owner of the person. This notion is well reflected in the writings of John Locke, who is regarded as an enormously influential figure for this worldview. Locke says,

> From all, which it is evident, that through the things of nature are given in common, yet man, by being master of himself, and proprietor of his own person, and the actions or labor of it, has still in himself the great foundation of property: and that, which made up the great part of what he applied to the support or comport of

his being, when invention and arts had improved the conveniences of life, was perfectly his own, and did not belong in common to others.[22]

To Locke, the individual is prior to society, which comes into existence only through the voluntary contract of individuals trying to maximize their own self-interest. In sum, the person in individualist cultures is defined apart from his or her specific collectives and contexts. M. Brinton Lykes calls this view of the person autonomous individualism.[23] Whether one's need for affiliation is high or low, the person is thought to be independent from others.

SHADES OF COMMUNALISM
IN RECENT WESTERN THOUGHT: COLLECTIVISM

The autonomous self is academia's primary focus in discussions about personhood, especially in psychology.[24] Communal personhood as understood by the majority of the world (Asians, Africans, and Latin Americans) is not taken seriously nor has it been a major player in academic discourse. Only recently have scholars started looking at communal personhood. For instance, Edward Sampson asserts that the autonomous individualistic notion of the self is an ahistorical and overbroad universalist understanding, one that ignores both the socio-historical context of the "subjects" and the social context that shapes the development of one's psychological wherewithal.[25]

Sampson argues that people shape their personhood in a particular context in which they live. Through interaction with others who share the values and ideology of a larger whole, a person internalizes those values and tries to be a desirable person, someone that society values. When they feel that they are accepted and valued by society, they have a positive self-concept. If they feel that they do not fit into the norms of society and are not valued, their self-concept becomes negative. This, then, brings focus to the problem as Sampson understands it, for autonomous individualism defines the person apart from his or her historical context; it describes the person as a self-contained, separate entity whose essence can be meaningfully abstracted from his or her relationships and contexts.[26] Arguably, the autonomous individualistic view of the person is not only incomplete, but it is an inauthentic understanding of the person. Hereto some of the dominant theories of psychology (e.g., Psychoanalytic Theory, Object Relation Theory,

Behaviorism, Cognitivism, Eriksonian Ego Identity Theory, and even the Humanistic Movement in psychology represented by Abraham Maslow) are based on a Western individualistic worldview, one that generalizes human nature anecdotally.[27]

Although the autonomous individualistic view of the person is a description of the person imagined solely by one particular constituency (namely, it is that of white, middle-class, college-educated males), it has become the universal understanding of the person.[28] The prevalence of this individualistic view of the person is associated with the Enlightenment, which sought to find a fundamental universality and a deep structure that all groups and, hence, individuals share.[29] With a universal norm also came an aversion to otherness and the differences suggested by it. Even though the Enlightenment sought far-reaching equality, Sampson insists that it was a homogenized one. Unless one shared the sameness of Western individualism, one was not equal. The views of women, people of color, and people of subordinate social class were excluded.

Today the Western world dominates the world intellectually, economically, and politically, so alternative anthropologies are short-changed. Accordingly, Sampson argues that the Western individualistic view of the person now is a means for maintaining a white, male status quo, one whose privilege is unwittingly supported by contemporary psychology.

As an alternative, some critics advocate a communal approach. Emphasizing the dialogic nature of the human person, Sampson insists that human nature is socially constructed in and through dialogues, conversations, and talk, and is therefore to be found only through relationships between and among people. There are no lone rangers when it comes to making meaning. Hereto, Sampson even suggests the shared ownership of self: "a person's interior is conversationally constituted and conversationally sustained. The presence of other is invariably involved."[30]

Echoing Sampson, philosopher Kathryn Addelson argues that nothing is completely independent in this world. Like Sampson, she also opines that an individualistic anthropology—one that reflects a male, Western, well-to-do worldview—dominates intellectual life.[31] Addelson submits that an individualistic perspective is a major obstacle to doing intellectually and morally responsible work in academia because it is so pervasive in higher education's epistemology, ethics, politics, and notion of truth and time. For example, in epistemology and ethics, an individualistic perspective leads a researcher to become a judging observer, an objective outsider, who is separated from time, place, social position, body, and intimate relations. This is a misunderstanding of the collective nature of human life, for even scientists, who seek objectivity, never do so without interacting with the world that they are studying. "Truth" is always against a backdrop of collective action that includes legislators passing laws and police and court officials enforcing them.[32] Every dimension of human social life is an outcome of what people do together. Individuals are products of collective action; they are inseparable from customs, norms, beliefs, and meanings. Hence, facts and truths are collectively enacted. Accordingly, one must utilize a collective philosophical anthropology to address human life fully.

Acknowledging the Western individualistic view's dominance and limitations is a good start. The next step will always be tricky, however, lest a communal-based worldview be communal only in name.[33] Korean psychologists Sang-Chin Choi and Soo-Hyang Choi argue that the concept of "collectivism," a term typically used in Western psychological literature to reference communal identity, bespeaks Western individualism. "[Collectivism] . . . appears to be formulated to conveniently provide an accentuating comparability to the Western individualistic framework."[34] According to Choi and Choi, one of the consistent themes associated with collectivism is its emphasis on group identity, which refers to a collection of individuals rather than to a group. Communalism as "many individuals" is an individualistic perspective, one that radically reshapes communal cultures' notion of personhood. The Western notion of communalism as a group ignores the contextual framework of communal societies; namely, it effectively voids the binding force and relationship that Korean "We-ness" discourse requires.[35]

The idea of community as a collection of individuals comes from individualists' understanding of "we" as the coexistence of independent "I" and "you." However, to a communalist, "I" and "you" are not individual units but, rather, a unified single entity.[36] Choi and Choi warn that an individualistically driven understanding of community is liable not only to turn the meaning of communal culture on its head but also to perpetuate witlessness about genuine cross-cultural differences, thereby perpetuating dominance of the individualistic perspective in the area of psychology, gussied up as "multiculturalism."[37]

CHURCH AS THERAPY?
OBSERVATIONS FROM THE BAY AREA

I asked a group of people who belong to a ChristCare group at a United Methodist church in suburban San Francisco to name the most representative feature of their small group. All of them said that the Christ-Care group is their weekly therapy session. One female member said,

> I am a quite successful lawyer. But the success comes with hard and stressful work. The ChristCare provides me a calm and non-competitive space that I don't find at work and home. I don't know how I can survive without this weekly "therapy" group meeting. These people know me and understand my hectic work and home life. Through praying with them, and doing a Bible study here every week, I gain encouragement and deeper faith.

When I asked the group's members whether they sacrifice time, energy, money, and personal freedom to help each other, they were silent for a while and smiled at each other. Then a member said that they always support each other, but no one could cite an instance except that they meet with each other weekly. Like Wuthnow's interviewees, members of this group help each other as long as their personal lives are not disrupted, and hence the misidentification of sacrifice with the act of meeting once a week. Privacy and personal life come before community.

This notion of community is a world apart from that of members of a Korean-American United Methodist church and a Tongan United Methodist church in the same area. Neither church has a ChristCare group. Unlike many mainline small groups that are driven by group members' needs or appetites, the members of the Korean and the Tongan churches belong to a class according to their residential district. As a class, they meet once a week for class prayer and fellowship. They meet not in the church, but at a member's home, which arguably provides a higher comfort level for newcomers. In their meetings, members talk about their past week's activities; about their concerns, hopes, sorrows, and joys. Generally a meal is served. As class members, they also participate in and take responsibilities for wide-ranging church activities. In the case of Koreans, each class takes a turn to provide lunch for the entire church every Sunday. Accordingly, they meet more than once a week. In addition to church activities, class members attend family ceremonial observance such as weddings, funerals, birthdays, and so on. Often households provide free childcare for other members, and they provide labor-laden services for other members such as preparing food for the aforementioned observances.

When asked to provide the best word to describe the meaning of the class, both Koreans and Tongans used "family." In fact, many Koreans refer to group members as family members. When asked whether a group like this is a burden, the response of a Korean woman summed up the typical response. She said that, "Yes, [belonging is a burden]. Once in a while it feels too much, but that is what family is about. We do it because we are family!"

This clearly suggests different concepts of community between the Anglo United Methodist small-group members and ethnic United Methodist class members. The Anglo members identify themselves collectively. They belong to and are dependent on their small group for personal fulfillment. Ironically, though, and from the standpoint of communal identity, the group is community only because it says so. There is no merging of egos incident to a larger purpose. People seek to fulfill individual needs and interests in a group setting. In this sense, the growing small-group movement of the mainline is rather promoting individualism than community. In fact, Wuthnow's reports conclude that one of the most salient features of American small groups is "Me-First religion":

> Group members are encouraged to think about the ways in which spirituality can help them, to apply faith concepts to their personal problems, and to share these problems with the group. In the process, it is easy for these practical, personal applications of faith to take precedence over everything.[38]

In most small groups, discussions, prayers, and studies are heavily focused on the needs and interests of individuals. Members are encouraged to understand a topic through the lens of their personal lives. To relate it to a larger whole and then back to themselves is seen as dogmatically impersonal. For example, Daniel Olson, who conducted an ethnographical research of a Disciple Bible study group at a United Methodist Church, reports that,

> Most of the life changes that group participants reported are of an inward, personal nature. During the interviews, six of the members told me that their participation in the Disciple program had given them a stronger faith, an inner peace, and a great ability to cope with stress.[39]

In sum, small-group ministries provide structure and environment for personal growth and communal support in a time-wise economical way. However, unlike one's expectation that small-group movements would transform individualism in mainline churches to a world-is-my-parish gospel, they strengthen individualism by promoting personal faith growth as an end in itself. As I do my research and listen to mainline Christian stories, there is much excitement for the potential change that small groups would bring to the church: that they purportedly are reintroducing community to the mainline. Yet I see them only promoting more individualism.

COMMUNAL WORLDVIEWS' POTENTIAL CONTRIBUTIONS

If the individualistic notion of community that prevails in mainline churches does not create and promote an authentic sense of community, what is the alternative? Where do we look for wisdom? Admittedly I emphasize different senses of community as culled from racial and ethnic mainline churches, so readers may think that my repertoire is too limited: that I should use communal worldviews and then some as models for mainline churches.

Communal cultures frame the interactive, group nature of human existence. Although communal cultures acknowledge human existence as a group endeavor, something which individualism misses, it admittedly has shortcomings. Since communal cultures require individuals to define themselves as part of the community, especially as members of the family, and thus to subordinate personal goals to those of the community, they hinder development of their own individuality and personhood. Moreover, the values of harmony and community that many communal societies emphasize are based on a hierarchical view of the person. The hierarchy of superior and inferior maintains the orderliness and harmony of power.[40] The superior partners have rights and duties of educating inferior partners, and the inferior partners have only obligations and no rights. In these hierarchical relationships, the inferior ones are forced to sacrifice for the value of harmony. Without their sacrifice, harmony is not possible. Therefore, it can be said that for inferior partners, the value of harmony ironically is a system of dehumanization and injustice.

Young Ae Kim, a Korean feminist, pastoral psychologist, finds low self-esteem among many Korean people as a result of communalism based on hierarchy.[41] The Korean communal sense of connectedness has less rigid ego boundaries, so that identification and projection of one person onto another occurs easily. When a person's ego faces that of another, there is ready identification with the other as one adapts one's own ego thus to orchestrate harmony. This tendency toward identification with others, especially with the powerful, forces people to align themselves with power and status. In other words, as culture inculcates respects between parties, the result is that of psychological dependency and lack of self-identity. Women, in particular, are forced to uphold patriarchy, but in doing so they lose their self-identity. An overemphasis on relatedness deprives Korean women of the power to know themselves, and it contributes to repressed feelings, diffused boundaries, low self-esteem, and dependency on others. Sacrificing one's needs for others' gain may result in anxiety about one's role in the universe, shame, and cluelessness about one's own talents and God's calling for oneself.

Communal cultures in general, and Korean society in particular, highly regard a person who is not very expressive—someone who is calm and prudent. The hierarchical and patriarchal social structure forces women and the powerless to be subordinate and silent. Silence blocks people from hearing their own voice, and the lack of power to know one's inner wisdom or knowledge forces one to defer to outer authority.[42] One becomes completely dependent on authority. If people hear their inner voices, they feel guilty toward persons in authority, as if they were depriving them of their power. Through this process, people in powerless situations not only lose their voices but also the power to claim their own raison d'etre. In other words, they are socialized into being dependent and powerless beings. Jean Baker Miller notes that while the powerful define the powerless as inferior, even the powerless cannot believe in their abilities. Because the powerless have to survive, they tend not to disturb the powerful.[43]

Communal cultures, which favor ingroup members over outgroup members, also create conflicts and antagonism among themselves.[44] One of the salient features of communalism is its clear distinction between ingroup and outgroup. Those who have "we" relations are considered members of the ingroup, and those who do not belong are members of the outgroups. The most prevalent "we" networks in communal societies are family, region, and school. "When people are connected through these networks, they treat others as members of 'we.' Once people are regarded as being within the boundary of 'we,' they incur instant closeness, assume social interdependence, and consequently give more favor to others in the group."[45] Accordingly, the more networks people share, the more smoothly business flows. Although the primary purpose of these networks is to promote good social relations, since they are only ingroup-centered networks, those networks often cause conflicts between ingroup and outgroup members of a communal society.

Such ingroup-centered networks not only create social favoritism, preventing outgroup members from having fair opportunities, but also hamper the process of forming society as a whole.[46] For instance, one of the most serious social problems in Korea is regional antagonism. Although it is a small country, people from three different regions, namely Kyungsango, Chonrado, and Choongchungdo, have had serious conflicts over many issues, especially about politics. Political parties are organized by people from the same region rather than by political positions, and national elections provide the opportunity to have people from the same region elected. Among laypeople, such regional conflicts are also prevalent. People from Chonrado and Kyungsango try to avoid establishing any possible relationships through marriages, job transfers, and so on. The Korean Psychological Association held several symposia on regional antagonism in Korea, the first being held in June 1988, under the theme, "The psychological viewpoint on regional antagonism in Korea." Korean social psychologists Kyung-Hwan Min and Hai-Sook Kim argue that regional antagonism in Korea is a pathological case of communalism that has created tension between ingroups and out-groups.[47] That is, although communalism itself is not to blame for intergroup conflict within a society, when the range of the ingroup is limited to a specific subgroup within a society, such as native region, rather than on a more superordinate level of category, such as the entire nation or humankind, it can result in pathological outgroup rejection and ingroup favoritism.

A model of community for the mainline needs a dual task: first, acknowledgment that a communal worldview celebrates our group relatedness; and, second, this model needs to challenge notions of community that would sacrifice one's sacred calling as an individual to social hierarchy and nepotism. In other words, a balance between communal culture's worldview and individualistic culture's stress on each person's novelty is an ideal pursuit for the mainline. I find such a balance in biblical models of community, which is the subject of the next two chapters.

SUGGESTED EXERCISE AND DISCUSSION TOPICS

Exercise: Tell Me about Your Family[48]

1. Have people get into two-member groups. One party will be A and the other will be B.
2. Give A and B the following instructions, respectively:

Instruction for A:

Tell your partner a particular story about your (extended) family from your childhood. After you finish, listen to your partner's family story. While your partner is telling his or her story, count how many times s/he uses these words—I, me, my, and mine. Your partner should not know that you are counting.

Instruction for B:

Your partner will tell you a story about his or her family from childhood. Listen to his or her story attentively. After your partner is done, tell him/her your own family story.

1. Ask A to tell B what A was doing and the number of times that B used "I" words.
2. Ask groups to reflect on their experiences.
3. Ask groups to retell the same family stories, this time using only "we" language.
4. Ask the groups to share their observations with one another.

Suggested Discussion Topics

1. What are some of the core characteristics of individualism, collectivism, and communalism? Name some examples. How are they similar to or different from each other?
2. Reflect on your faith community, especially on a particular program intended to build community. Name five characteristics of the program. Compare them to the characteristics that you named in number 1. What is the nature of the "community" in your faith communities? How is it helping or hindering?

Chapter 2

A Biblical Call to Communal Faith and Ministry

Learning from the Hebrew Bible

Each fall I co-teach two classes with a Protestant spirituality scholar: Spiritual Disciplines for Leadership and Teaching Protestant Spiritual Disciplines in Communities of Faith. Both courses are based on Protestant spirituality; they are earmarked for entering Master of Divinity students. Although most of our students come from different Protestant backgrounds, each year students tell us that they are not familiar with Protestant spirituality, and some students find the concept oxymoronic. Many Protestant students have familiarity with Roman Catholic traditions or Eastern religions, but the spirituality of their Protestant forebears (e.g., Luther's Four-Stranded Garland Prayer and John Wesley's Covenant Group) is new.[1] I find a similar cluelessness to discussions about biblical community in mainline churches. We naturally use the social sciences, business models, and marketing strategies for community development but are less fluent with the biblical writers' struggles with and cultivation of community. The biblical notion of community presupposes communal existence; it also emphasizes the accountability and individuality of each person in the community. In the following section I invite readers to explore a biblical sense of community as reflected in the notion of a people for God. My goal is to broaden our repertoire of tools so that "knowledge and vital piety" can shape and reshape our corporate spirituality.[2]

WHO ARE THE PEOPLE OF GOD?

Who are the People of God? How were they formed as a people? Where were they from? These are crucial questions to ask for the examination of biblical community. Depending on how one answers these questions, the People of God can be a foundation for both individualistic exclusivism and communal inclusivism.

Among the four major theories of the origin of Israel examined below, the Military Conquest Theory and the Peasant Revolution Theory emphasize communal inclusivism among established community members and an exclusionary attitude toward outsiders. On the other hand, the Peaceful Infiltration Theory and Archaeological Approach are more inclusive of outsiders conceptually and emphasize the accountability of each person within the existing—albeit ever-changing—community.

Scholars of ancient Israel are divided over almost every aspect of its origins, background(s), relationships with the Canaanite population, and processes of settlement.[3] Regarding the People of God's origins, for instance, the Military Conquest Theory and Peasant Revolution Theory prevailed until the early 1960s and speculated that the People of God migrated westward from the desert. In terms of the manner of their settlement, William F. Albright and his school theorize a military conquest, as suggested by Joshua: A unified military assault by well-organized groups, emerging from the desert in a series of well-coordinated attacks, thence destroying the mighty Canaanite city-states. George E. Wright describes the events of the military conquest as following:

> The manifold evidence for the terrific destruction suffered by the cities of Bethel, Lachish, Eglon, Debir (Kiriath sepher), and Hazor during the 13th century certainly suggests that a planned campaign such as that depicted in Josh. 10–11 was carried out. . . . We may

safely conclude that during the 13th century a portion at least of the later nation of Israel gained entrance to Palestine by a carefully planned invasion.[4]

Although Albrecht Alt agrees with the Albright school that the People of God came from the desert, he argues for a peaceful infiltration of pastoralists—perhaps the Shosu and *'Apiru* of Egypt, into the sparsely populated regions of Canaan.[5] According to Alt, the process of settlement took place over a long period of time as the nomads annually moved back and forth between the desert fringe of Transjordan for wintering and the central hill country for summering. This search for pasturage repeated itself year after year, until the nomads began to transfer the focus of their activities to the settled areas, creating a network of agreements with the inhabitants.

Regarding the obviously military invasion stories in the Pentateuch, Alt and his followers say that those stories were actually the descriptions of a later stage of the settlement process. When the biblical descriptions were redacted during the Monarchy, memories of the wars of expansion were still fresh. And since most of the territory was acquired in those military campaigns, they were associated with the initial stage of Israelite settlement. According to Alt, the story of Israelite settlement was dramatized during the period of the Monarchy.[6]

The Peasant Revolution Model, which emerged in the late 1950s, rejects any eastern desert origin of the People of God. Norman Gottwald and George Mendenhall instead advocate that the Israelites were the oppressed lower class of urban Canaan who rebelled and carried out an armed struggle against the ruling class.[7] The People of God arose as a revolutionary movement among those who already inhabited Canaan. Refusing to pay tribute to the cities' rulers and their oppressive cultic potentates, these revolutionary peasants consciously flocked to and embraced a new god, Yahweh, seen as the god of the oppressed.[8] In short, unlike the eastern desert origin views, the sociologically based schools opine that the basic conflict in the land of Israel was not between the desert and the town, or between shepherd and farmer; rather it was between the oppressed and the oppressors.

These models are either rejected wholesale or challenged by biblical archaeologists who bring a whole new perspective, one that radically challenges traditional approaches.[9] Based on excavation, the survey of material culture, especially pottery and architecture, ecological data and ethnographic studies of Palestine, biblical archaeologists, especially

Israel Finkelstein, present three new points:[10] First, the formation and settlement of Israel was a gradual one starting from the sixteenth century BCE.

Second, the confederating process was a regional phenomenon. Most settlers were indigenous nomads who sparsely inhabited "frontier zones" that were suitable for pasturage, such as the Transjordan Plateau, the Jordan Valley, the desert fringe, and the hill country. Although some of the settlers were from outside the country, including the eastern desert and the coastal plain, the majority of the settlers were local nomads, ones that had a symbiotic relationship with the city dwellers in Canaan.[11] Although pottery types and architectural structures found in the Canaanite cities and the hill regions show a certain connection between the two, their distinctive features do not support the peasant revolutionary model.

And third, the biblical depiction of the rise of early Israel, such as stories of the Patriarchs, Exodus, and Conquest, was recast by the Deuteronomic historians to serve their ideology and historical-national convictions. The description constituted a "mythical memory of a Golden age" produced by orthodox, nationalist reform parties during the Assyrian crisis in the brief reign of Josiah, late in Judah's history.[12]

Among these conflicting theories about the People of God's origins, contemporary biblical scholarship's debates increasingly focus on and are defined by biblical archaeology's arguments.[13] According to Jeffrey Kuan, a prominent Hebrew Bible scholar, such an approach not only has material evidence to support its points but also is a more liberating approach resonating with liberationist biblical hermeneutics suggested by feminists, post-modernists, and post-colonialists.[14] Since the archaeological approach presents the origin and the settlement of the People of God as different groups becoming a people over a long period of time, its quest is to figure out workable relationships and appropriate socio-political-religious systems. It thus presents an image of God for all people, not just for certain chosen people; it proffers a communal anthropology, a broad concept of community, and the importance of accountability of each person as a member of a community. Such an approach works handsomely with liberationist biblical scholarship, the passion of which is to highlight God's justice and love for all people by lifting up the silenced voices of the marginalized and to analyze their struggles for self-determination by problematizing the authority of the text and emphasizing the importance of readers' responses, the contexts of the text and its writers' hermeneutics.

Notwithstanding this, some theologians, especially Native American scholars, assert that the God of Exodus—a crucial player in both traditionalist and liberationist hermeneutics—is not a God of justice.[15] To Native Americans, who identify themselves with Canaanites, Exodus is a story about invasion. The God of Exodus is an unjust and brutal God who saves certain people at the expense of others. Arguably these positions are irreconcilable; to debate them further or find a *via media* exceeds this chapter's focus except to acknowledge that they exist and are weighty issues.

The above research of archaeology and liberationist hermeneutics suggests a different direction for the study of the People of God. The People of God was a community formed by different groups of natives over a long period of time. Key biblical narratives later were idealized and canonized. Therefore study of the People of God should look at the characteristics of the community rather than primarily at chronological developments since these are largely shaped by ideology. Accordingly I now analyze the features of the community and its covenants. I particularly am interested in whether the biblical account(s) emphasizes community over individuals or whether it promotes each person's individuality.

THE PEOPLE OF GOD AND THE COMMUNITY

The People of God affirms human nature as communal, as communalists do (Chapter 1), and at the same time strongly promotes each person's individuality.

Joseph Shaw emphasizes the importance of the communalist approach to the People of God.[16] As examined in Chapter 1, individualists and communalists have very different concepts of community. To individualists, community generally means a collection of individuals. A human being is viewed as an autonomous, independent entity, and accordingly, "we" is understood as the coexistence of "I" and "you." However, the person in communal societies is an interdependent and interconnected being who even shares ego boundaries with others. "I" and "you" are not individual units; rather they are a unified single unity.[17] This communal view is the personhood that the People of God evokes.

"[T]he People of God does not mean a random plurality of individuals," Shaw asserts, "but a particular, corporate entity, a given community."[18] It is not a collection of scattered individuals who claim to have some special relationship to God, but the entire community as a whole and as committed to God. The individual has life only as a member of the corporate whole. As in contemporary communal societies, it is not the individual, but the family, the clan, the tribe, or the nation that is the basic unit of the society. For example, when Achan, the son of Carmi, took forbidden spoil, Joshua says, "The people of Israel broke faith" (7:1). Israel is the people as a whole; in other words, it has a corporate identity. The tragedy of the rupture between Ephraim and Judah was not forgotten (Isaiah 7:17), for the prophets looked forward to the day when Israel's unity would be restored (Ezekiel 37:15–19). H. Wheeler Robinson observes that modern Western thought erroneously interprets such texts individualistically and treats the single individual as the unit (e.g., for punishment or reward), whereas ancient Hebrews envisaged the whole community as the unit.[19]

Regarding individual hero narratives, such as the calls of Abraham and Moses, Shaw asserts that we should understand them as stories about instrumental individuals helping to extend divine blessings to all the peoples of the earth.[20] For example, the call of Abraham in Genesis 12:3-12 is not simply the story about a promising individual singled out by God for a saintly career; rather Abraham (or Abram) is chosen as the human instrument through whom God will bestow blessings on "all the families of the earth." In the post-exile literature, such stories of instrumental individuals are expanded to a much larger scale. Now Israel becomes the instrument for God's blessings to all humankind.

Both the People of God and contemporary communalism often emphasize the importance of community over individuals, but there still is a big difference in their views about individuality. In communal societies, members are encouraged to think of goals and interests of the community before they pursue their personal goals and interests. As examined in Chapter 1, if there are conflicts between the two, individual members are expected to suppress their personal interests and are even forced to sacrifice themselves for the sake of the community. In such communal societies, people have fewer opportunities and less encouragement to develop their own individuality, which often results in low self-esteem.[21] The sense of connectedness that communal societies highly value creates less rigid ego boundaries so that identification and projection of one person onto another occurs easily. When a person's ego faces that of another, there is ready identification with the other by taking on similarities or by sidestepping differences. This tendency toward identification with others, especially with the powerful, forces people to show their best to identify themselves with more powerful and higher status persons. That is, in the name of social harmony, communal societies often perpetuate strong dependency and lack of self-identity.

However, this is not the case in the People of God. According to Christopher Wright, who studied individual and communal ethics in the Hebrew Bible, community-oriented ethics, especially in the notion of the People of God, does not disregard one's individuality nor does it displace personal responsibility.[22] Despite all its emphasis on the communal aspect, the idea of the People of God never loses sight of the importance of each person's individuality: Different groups of natives forged a common sense of origin and identity through literally and figuratively wrestling with Yahweh (e.g., Genesis 32:22–32), rather than through ideology.[23] Thus having Yahweh as the initiator of the community, they identified themselves as the People of God so that no individualized groups' self-interests had timeless hegemony.

In such a community, each member is constantly reminded of the importance of the God-centered community with its rituals, covenants, and laws. However, without the commitment and willingness of each member, the community could not maintain its identity and health. Therefore, each person's individuality is also highlighted. Without their own individuality, members could easily be lost to ideological mean-dering and thus lose vision and purpose. This is the reason why the notion of the People of God throughout the Hebrew Bible never soft-pedals personal responsibility. Whenever the People of God lost its purpose as the Godward community and just became a nation or set of systems, prophets challenged and reminded them of their identity as the People of God.[24] Although the term *Israel*, which is a more visualized term for the People of God's relation to God, later became the name of the northern state, prophets like Amos and Hosea often used it for both states to emphasize the entire community's relation to God.

In sum, unlike a communalism that expects each member to give up on their individuality for the unity of community, the biblical communalism reflected in the People of God considers individuality as a key for communal harmony. The two constitute an oxymoronic ethos. Samuel Newell, Jr., summarizes such a relationship as follows:

> In the Old Testament documents the community and the individual bear to one another just such a fluid relationship. A thoroughly self-consistent concept of religion as a group experience, to the rigid exclusion of all individual experience, was impossible in the Old

Testament, even as in the New Testament we shall find that a thoroughly self-consistent individualism, without an equally weighty group concern, was neither possible nor desirable.[25]

BIBLICAL COVENANTS: LIVING AS A COMMUNITY

Such a fluid relationship between individuality and community was also prevailing in rules of community life that were presented in the form of covenant. The covenant in general has two major forms: 1) the covenant with God the initiator and the center of the community—faithfulness; 2) the covenant between people—compassion.[26] Both forms of the covenant uphold community as the foundation and emphasize individuality simultaneously.

Like the notion of community, the essence of the covenant with God is communal: "I shall be your God; you shall be my people."[27] Here "you" and "your" are plural. That is, God the initiator of the community is not just making covenant with certain representative individuals but with the entire community composed of many different groups of people. Using such a rhetorical form, the covenant makes itself very clear that harmony and well-being of the community is more important than individual interests.

Seymour Siegel, a Jewish biblical scholar, explains this point in connection with the notion of *shalom*.[28] The Godward community should reflect God's presence in its character, determine its destiny, and guarantee its future. The biblical ideal for such a stage is *shalom,* whose fundamental meaning is totality, a harmonious community as a whole where the untrammeled and free growth of every soul is guaranteed.[29] That is, the covenant, which is a confirmation of the spirit of God among the people, is also a guarantee of *shalom.* From the outset, the covenant makes clear that fidelity to Yahweh means compassion for the neighbor: "Infractions of Yahweh's will were never simply private offenses; they were assaults on the integrity and well-being of the community."[30] This is the reason why the words *berith* (covenant) and *shalom* in the Hebrew Bible are often used interchangeably (Ezekiel 34:25; 37:26). In sum, to enter the covenant means that the entire community makes a commitment to harmonious living together with God and God's people, because God's purpose is not just righteous individuals but a new community who in their life should embody *shalom.* Throughout the Hebrew Scriptures the same message is repeated over and over again.

Although the foundation and emphasis of the covenant is communal, as was the notion of the community, the primary demand of the covenant is addressed to each individual member, with a singular "you": "You shall have no other gods before me" (Exodus 20:3). The same is true of the rest of the Decalogue, and of a substantial number of the detailed laws of the Pentateuch. The earliest law code (Exodus 21–23, for example) operates legislatively on the unmistakable ground of individual responsibility and liability before the law.[31] Although the covenant was established between God and the entire community, without each member's commitment the purpose of the covenant would not be accomplished, and its implications affected not only the community but also every person within it. Christopher Wright summarizes the relationship between the community and the individual within it as follows:

> If God desired a society characterized by economic equality and compassion, then it required individuals to forget selfishness and resist the temptation to cash in unjustly on the misfortunes of a neighbor. If he wanted a society founded on justice and ordered by laws known and upheld, then it was up to individual judges to act impartially and incorruptibly. And so one could go through the whole spectrum of social characteristics, drawing out their individual entailments.[32]

That is, the individuality of each person enables her to be an accountable member of the Godward community. The communal and individual are in many ways inseparable in the covenant.

The importance of individuality is a strong theme of many prophets. For example, Isaiah repeatedly emphasizes the concept of remnants through whom God carries out God's purpose. When the larger community lost its purpose as God's people and uncritically adopted political nation-building, Isaiah stood in opposition:

> Asserting that out of the nation there should be chosen, on the basis of individual loyalty to the covenant, certain individuals who together would form the righteous remnant, and who would accomplish, throughout Yahweh's help, the thing for which the nation had shown itself unfit.[33]

The community composed of politically driven conformists was not the Godward community any longer; it no longer could carry on God's purpose because it esteemed like-mindedness.

Isaiah was not the only prophet who advocated individuality relative to communal conformity. Most prophets fundamentally were individualists.[34] They refused to be silenced and instead unashamedly maintained the individuality of their position, reminding others of their lost identity as God's people.[35] In sum, a community cannot be an authentic community without individuality. In the Hebrew Bible, community and individual are inseparable, and both are covenantal. When the fluid or reciprocal relations between the two are broken, neither the community nor the individual can maintain itself.

It is clear that the notion of the People of God emphasizes both community and individuality. It starts from and upholds humankind's communal nature and advocates each person's individuality. The notion of the People of God straightforwardly rejects communal exclusivism and challenges conformity. Although the People of God emphasizes each person's individuality to help the community keep its identity, that does not mean it supports individualism. In fact, it is what biblical community completely challenges.

Such notion of a community challenges a widespread view that the Bible speaks about the chosen people based on exclusive election theology. Many people, including both Christians and Jews, have interpreted the concept of the People of God in an arrogant, bigoted, self-righteous sense as a way of exalting themselves above other peoples.[36] However, the notion of the People of God reviewed in this chapter emphatically rejects such a view. The origin of the People of God itself tells us that they were composed of many different groups of natives. Building and maintaining a healthy Godward community was their primary concern. Subsequently, the theological boundary of the People of God was expanded from their own community to the entire world, which also became the recipient of God's grace. According to Gerhard Lohfink, the sequence of the Hebrew Bible itself clearly shows such universalism:

> The Bible does not begin with the election of the people of God, but with the creation of the world. Its first figure is not Abraham, but the 'adam, the human being, and in the first chapters of Genesis 'adam refers not to a particular individual, but to humanity as a whole. The Bible begins with humanity. God's concern is not first of all for Israel, but for the whole world.[37]

Since each person's accountability based on their own individuality is essential to keep the community from conformity, the People of God has far-reaching implications. As God's people, Israel's concern is to follow God's purpose, which is to transform the world by giving witness to the Torah, God's social order.[38] In this sense, Daniel Harrington insists that the election of Israel should be understood as a vocation to be a light to the entire world. Israel's recognition of itself as God's people supersedes exclusive nationalism.[39] Moreover, Harrington suggests that those Jewish writings from the so-called postexilic or intertestamental periods, which emphasize particular commandments (such as prohibition of mixed marriages, circumcision of males, etc.) should be understood as Jewish efforts to keep their identity and ensure consciousness of belonging to God's people in a cosmopolitan milieu.[40] They are not antagonistic per se to outsiders, in other words.

Despite such interpretations, reinterpretations, and clarifications of the notion of the People of God, one fundamental question remains: The story of the People of God is an invasion story that has explicitly and implicitly been used to justify imperialism and other forms of oppression. For example, relying on texts like the Exodus, many Christian believers entered and took the lands of non-Christian Asians and Africans either to convert them or to promote self-serving claims of superiority and election.[41] The text not only has its own historical world and environment but also "travels in the world and participates in history, continuing to write its story far beyond its original context and readers."[42] Accordingly, it is crucial for any reader of the Bible to reinterpret the text in its own context, thus to challenge oppressive ideologies and to proclaim God's life-giving message for all. I will delve into this subject in Chapter 7.

SUGGESTED EXERCISE AND DISCUSSION TOPICS

Exercise: A Guided Imagery and Meditation Exercise (Joshua 7:1–26)

Read the story of Achan from the Book of Joshua, chapter 7. Then read through the story again slowly. This time, pause after each phrase and imagine the scene. Close your eyes and open your imagination.

1. Slowly read verses 1–9. Explore this scene fully. What is the setting? What are the sounds, sights, and aromas? Who else is there? What do they look like? What do their faces tell you?
2. Slowly read verses 10–15. Imagine yourself as a part of the crowd. Where are you in the crowd? What did you hear? How do

you feel? What are your physical, emotional, and spiritual reactions to the story?

3. Slowly read verses 16–26. Now the story is concluded. Do you stay there? Do you go elsewhere? With whom do you talk about what you saw?

4. What is the story's meaning for you now? What do you think of God's punishment of everyone for Achan's sin? What is the relationship between an individual member and the community here? What is the meaning of this relationship for your faith community?

Suggested Discussion Topics

1. How have you learned and understood the meaning of the People of God?

2. Does your faith community have a clear idea of community grounded in the biblical tradition? Do you think the People of God can serve as a biblical foundation for your church's community building? Why or why not?

3. Reflect on the dynamics between an individual member and the entire community as suggested in the notions of the People of God, shalom, and the covenant. Compare your church's dynamics to those of the Bible, and discuss its challenges and affirmations for you and your community.

Chapter 3

A Biblical Community in the New Testament

The Body of Christ

There has been no other metaphor used more than the Body of Christ to describe the nature of the church throughout Christian history. At the same time, Dennis Jacobsen argues that the Body of Christ known by modern Christians is "distorted almost beyond recognition."[1] In other words, as much as the Body of Christ has been popularized, various interpretations have been given to its meaning. In this chapter, I offer another interpretation focusing on community.

THE NOTION OF COMMUNITY
REFLECTED IN THE BODY OF CHRIST

The notion of the People of God is continued in the New Testament.

There it is reinterpreted and expanded by Paul, who mostly worked with Gentile Christians living in a Hellenized world.[2] For example, in Romans 9:25, Paul quotes Hosea 2:23: "Those who were not my people I will call 'my people,' and he who was not beloved I will call 'beloved.'" Paul's emphasis here is not on the relationship between God and Israel, the People of God by birth, but on that of God to Gentiles that now are Christian, God's people by those individuals' choice.[3] In other words, Paul continues what was proposed by Daniel Harrington in the previous section: That the People of God consists of the entire world, including both Jews and Gentiles. Therefore, Gentile Christians are legitimately God's people, ones who have equal rights and responsibility to Jews.

Paul not only articulates the notion of the People of God in Christian contexts but also suggests the analogy of the Body of Christ to deliver a similar message to Gentile Christians. Utilizing the image of body, which is a popular Hellenistic concept, Paul particularly offers his view of Christian existence: To be a Christian is to be incorporated in a community of persons in which the individual belongs to Christ and to one another.[4]

Describing such existence as diversity within unity, Paul emphasizes both communal existence as humankind's fundamental nature and the importance of each person's individuality. In other words, like the notion of the People of God, the Body of Christ rejects both radical individualism and communalism as either/or. In the following section, I investigate the notion of community and challenge any interpretation that understands the Body of Christ as a fellowship *between* Christians or *between* same-church members.

PAUL'S MINISTRY WITH GENTILES IN THE HELLENISTIC CONTEXT

Conflicts among Gentile Christians

The concept of the Body of Christ is the product of Paul's ministry with newly converted Gentile Christians living in a heavily Hellenized world.[5] For example, in the city of Corinth the Romans were the dominant group, but since the Roman world including Corinth had been thoroughly Hellenized, the city also had strong Greek influences in its daily conventions, religion, philosophy, the arts, and so on.[6] Accordingly, most converted Christians also brought with them their Greek ways of life and thoughts: They approached the Christian faith and community life with Hellenistic worldviews, ethical norms, practices, and even religious traditions, under the aegis of Roman rule, which also influenced their worldview.

However, those Hellenistic Christians were not a homogeneous group, but, rather, people from diverse cultural, religious, social, and class backgrounds. Moreover, depending on their social classes, they had very different worldviews and religious ideas.[7] In the Corinthian church, for instance, the majority of church members were from the lower classes, including some slaves (I Corinthians 7:21–24). There were only a few wealthy and upper-class families in the church, and they were probably influenced by Cynic and Stoic philosophy.[8] Notwithstanding that, these wealthy Christians were the minority, yet they still tried to impose their upper-class norms on the majority of lower-class members. Hence there were serious conflicts between these two groups. Dale Martin insists that many issues addressed in I Corinthians—such as the Lord's supper, eating meat offered to idols, internecine lawsuits, and reactions to Paul's self-support through manual labor—are evidences of such conflicts.[9] Hereto, Paul challenged both groups and taught ideal Christian existence through the analogy of the Body of Christ.

The Hellenistic Ideology of Body

Among many other metaphors, why does Paul use this particular metaphor, the Body of Christ? According to Dale Martin, it is because the conflict between the two groups described above is rooted in the Hellenistic view of the body, which is a pinion of social harmony based on hierarchy.[10] The body ideology consists of two fundamental beliefs: 1) there is hierarchy in the human body; 2) there is cardinal continuity between human body and social body, and, therefore, hierarchy is part of the natural social order.[11] Some Greeks believed that parts of the human body like the head were more important than other parts, and that the social body, a macrocosm of the human body, evidences similar qualities. Hence inequality and hierarchy are necessary elements of social order.[12] Tampering with this system could bring disaster to cosmic harmony, so the hierarchical boundaries between free and slave, between male and female, and between Greeks and non-Greeks should be maintained. The upper class that enjoyed its wealth and power thus was continued, even in the local church.[13]

Martin argues that this conception of the body is exactly what those upper-class members brought to the Corinthian church.[14] For example, the wealthy members were accustomed to the conventions of the upper-class society and naturally expected status differentiation at church. They were also people who could afford to buy meat in the market, almost all of which would have been sacrificed to some deity before sale. The total avoidance of meat was difficult for them since they needed to give and receive dinner invitations from Corinth's elite. Accordingly, the well-to-do demanded status recognition and flexibility in the rules, thus saying, "All things are lawful for me" (6:12; 10:23), and "Food is meant for the stomach and the stomach for food" (6:13).

On the other hand, the lower-class members of Corinth's church were attracted to a Christian gospel that proclaimed God's love for all and challenged the existing social order, so they refused the continuation of social hierarchy by the upper-class members within the church.[15] Consequently, conflicts between the two groups were inevitable.

Paul envisioned a new community and opposed the hierarchical worldview of the upper-class members: He clearly and unambiguously took the side of the weak.[16] He urged the higher-status Christians to change their attitudes in ways that supported the position of the lower-status Christians; to wit, by imitating Paul's own self-lowering and status reversal. In other words, Paul advocated what upper-class ideology fears the most: disruption of the hierarchical social order/body.[17] He explicitly and implicitly emphasized that the Christian community is a new community in which no one seeks one's own honor, but, rather, one associates with the lowly and gives honor to others: "Live in harmony with one another; do not be haughty, but associate with the lowly; do not claim to be wiser than you are" (Romans 12:16). It is an alternative, countercultural community in which all existing social, cultural, religious, and gender divisions and differences should be overcome.[18]

THE BODY OF CHRIST: PAUL'S INTERPRETATION OF THE BODY, A RADICALLY NEW COMMUNITY

For the Christian community, a countercultural community, Paul suggests an alternative body ideology, one from the perspective of the marginalized: The Body of Christ.[19] In Romans 12:4–5 and I Corinthians 12:12–27, Paul offers the image of the body, emphasizing diversity in unity rather than the hierarchical ideology of the Hellenistic world. The human body is composed of many different parts having widely different functions. Yet, as one body it is a single functional unit, and all of its members work harmoniously for the good of the whole. Although the members of the body need to recognize that each has a different function, each also needs to recognize that none could survive without the others: "Individually we are members one of another" (Romans 12:5); "If one member suffers, all suffer together with it" (I Corinthians 12:26). Through the parable of the parts of the body speaking to each other about the need of each other, Paul strongly stresses mutuality and interdependence of body members. Independence, isolation, arrogance, and selfishness have no place in this new body ideology: There is functional differentiation but no hierarchical division.[20]

Paul extends the above human body analogy into a social body from a Christian perspective. Identifying the church as the Body of Christ, he emphasizes that the Body of Christ is a community in which each Christian is a real member of Christ's actual body; in which each Christian has different abilities and spiritual gifts; and in which all Christians are equal with merely functional differences.[21] As the human body needs many parts to function, the church also needs the gifts and abilities of all of its members. All the gifts that different members have—such as wisdom, knowledge, healing, miracles, prophecy, discernment, tongues, interpretation, serving, teaching, encouraging, giving, leadership, and showing mercy—are bestowed by the same Spirit.[22] They are all necessary and equally important gifts for the well-being of the whole Body of Christ. All depend on each other in this great diversity of gifts. In short, unlike the Hellenistic concept of the body, the Christian community as a new body should be based on radical egalitarianism in which everyone works side by side for the common good.[23]

With the image of the church as the Body of Christ, Paul makes essentially two points for the ideal Christian existence: the necessity of unity and the necessity of diversity.[24] The key to the unity is common experience in the Spirit (I Corinthians 12:13). Whether Jew or Greek, male or female, slave or free (Galatians 3:27–28), all are one in Christ through the Spirit.[25]

Precisely because they are one in Christ, the rich must stop discriminating against the poor at the Lord's table (I Corinthians 11:22, 29); and those who are more visible in their abilities and functions should not say to the less visible, "We have no need of you" (I Corinthians 12:21–26). As the human body cannot be torn into pieces, the church as a body cannot be broken down into individual parts without severe injury both to the church and to its members. God has so arranged the body that all the members are essential to one another. Accordingly, unity, the solidarity in Christ, and communality are the essential mode of the Christian Church.[26]

However, Paul's strong emphasis on the necessity of unity for the well-being of the church does not undermine diversity within it at all:

> For just as the body is one and has many members, and all the members of the body, though many, are one body, so it is with Christ. For in the one Spirit we were all baptized into one body— Jews or Greeks, slaves or free—and we were all made to drink of one Spirit. Indeed, the body does not consist of one member but of many. (I Corinthians 12:12–14)

Gordon Fee points out that Paul's primary concern here is not the priority of unity over diversity, since the body is one; rather Paul puts great emphasis on the necessity of diversity.[27] Even though the body is one, it does not consist of one member but of many. Therefore, unity without diversity does not make a community healthy. More concretely, in the context of the Corinthian church, Paul urges that those higher-class members recognize they all need the varied gifts of one and the same Spirit. The singular focus on one gift—whether it be wisdom, knowledge, prophecy, tongues, or interpretations—harms the health of the body and eventually leads to death. Therefore, the strong must stop disregarding the weak as less important than themselves: "The church as the 'Body of Christ' is its essential unity within its obvious diversity."[28]

THE NATURE OF COMMUNITY IN THE IMAGE OF THE BODY OF CHRIST

Through the image of the church as the Body of Christ, Paul also suggests a desirable human relationship. In several places, such as I Corinthians 12:13 and Galatians 3:27, Paul opines that to be a Christian is to be "baptized into one body," and "to be baptized into Christ" is equated with being in the church.[29] In other words, to be a Christian is to be a new creation and to be part of a larger whole at the same time.

As stated above, the church was a radically different community from the hierarchical society of the Hellenistic world.[30] Paul repeats over and over again that within the Christian community, no structures of dominance and division—such as Jews against Greek, slave against free, male against female—should be tolerated. All of the baptized are equal and one in Christ. This egalitarianism requires interdependence, mutuality, and respect for others' gifts and abilities. Since each person is a part of the one body, Christ, each member knows the humility of receiving their gifts from Christ (I Corinthians 12:12). Women and men, free and slave, Jews and Greeks in the Christian community are not defined by their sexual, religious, cultural, or social roles but by their discipleship and oneness with one another.[31]

Like the People of God, such egalitarianism challenges both individualism and communalism. Although the Body of Christ strongly emphasizes the necessity of unity, it is very critical of a communalism that rules out the importance of each person's individuality in the name of communal harmony. According to Fika van Rensburg, the reason why Paul pays great attention to both unity and diversity is to prevent unity from becoming uniformity.[32] Without individuality, it is too difficult for Christians to claim and keep their identity as new creations of God in a world that often defines people based on class, sex, and race. Individuality coupled with commitment to the well-being of others makes each person a responsible partner of a larger whole. If the body's unity results in destroying individuality, then the unity is no longer unity; rather it is totalitarianism gussied up as unity: "The lesser totality exists, then, in dynamic relation to the greater without losing its distinctive individuality."[33]

However, such emphasis on individuality should not be confused with autonomous, independent, and isolated individualism. In fact, Paul sees individualism as inauthentic existence that has nothing to do with Christian personhood.[34] The individual in the Body of Christ does not have real existence apart from the whole. Van Rensburg points out that the unity that the Body of Christ presents is not a mechanical unity but, rather, an organic one.[35] The parts of the body are not only constitutive of the body but also interdependent on each other. Every individual is equally important and is required to contribute to the well-being of the whole body. Nurturing an individual relationship with Christ as an autonomous and independent person is not authentic self-actualization because being a Christian is to be a part of Christ's body with other members. James Breed summarizes such communal nature as follows:

> There is no isolation among Christians, nor is there such thing as an essentially independent Christian congregation. The personal union with Christ also involves incorporation in the collective Christian society.[36]

Each person is expected to become a responsible partner of Christ and one another. Or as Jerome Murphy-O'Connor says, "Faith is the choice of a mode of being that is essentially social. Faith is a new way of being with others."[37]

In sum, the Body of Christ upholds humankind's communal nature and each person's individuality simultaneously. Neither diversity without unity nor unity without diversity is healthy. Likewise, neither the person separated from the community nor the community ignoring its member's individuality is an authentic existence. Only community that respects each member's individuality is equipped to protect itself from the danger of conformity and individualism. What insights and challenges does the above examination of the Body of Christ hold for the contemporary mainline churches?

First, it challenges a worldview that upholds the communal nature of human existence but does not recognize each person's individuality. A community that is composed of people without their own individuality cannot be the accountable and countercultural community that God calls the Christian church to be in the Body of Christ. In the Body of Christ, women and men, free and slave, Jews and Greeks are called to be new creations, not defined by their sexual, religious, cultural, or social roles. As the powerful are parts of the Christ's body and expected to contribute to the well-being of the body through their particular gifts, so are women and the poor. Paul emphasizes that privileges based on class, gender, and economic status are no longer valid. Everybody is allowed to exercise leadership functions in the community. As Yong Ting Jin, an Asian feminist theologian, emphasizes,

> Each person has a unique and creative role to play as inspired and sustained by the Spirit. Everyone is charismatic, no one is useless. As such, each member has a decisive place in the community, but all serving one another, all having and enjoying equal dignity.[38]

Second, Paul cautions against barriers between peoples, for too often they are the genesis of self-serving isolationism. A Christianity located in the midst of multiple world religions, some of which predate Christianity, is wrongheaded to refuse engagement. This exclusivism is based on an ideological hierarchy that one's own church, denomination, or religion is better than others. It is exactly what Paul urged the early Christians to challenge when he called them to become a countercultural community in a hierarchically ordered Hellenistic world. As modern Christians we should revisit the meaning of the Body of Christ so that we can broaden what sometimes would appear to be a self-involved and radically truncated worldview.

FURTHER QUESTIONS TO EXPLORE

Although the Body of Christ suggests a holistic view of the world, community, and personhood, emphasizing both unity and diversity, biblical scholars note that Paul's letters contain many contradictory statements and practices. Some feminist theologians point out that Paul advocates nonhierarchical models of community and human relationship, but when it comes to male-female relations, his attitude is hegemonic, man over woman.[39] In other words, in practice, Paul's Body of Christ could never be fully implemented because of an inherent flaw.

Postcolonial theologians raise other questions regarding Paul's attitude toward other religions. For example, Musa Dube insists that Paul's writings—despite the anachronism of the argument—are a policy statement for Christian imperialism.[40] In Galatians 4:8, Paul calls those newly converted Christians those who "were enslaved to beings that by nature are not gods." Paul thus apparently opines that Christianity is the only true religion, one that is superior to other religions. Dube argues that this attitude is prevalent throughout the New Testament and that it was later coupled with Reformation theology and then spread to other parts of the world by Western eighteenth- and nineteenth-century missionary movements.[41] This observation ironically makes one of my points; namely, the Christian worldview is indeed that: perspectives, ideas, experiences, observations, toned cogitation, and freewheeling insights. These sometimes appear mismatched. *Oisgepetch* comes to mind. This is Yiddish phraseology for when one "gussies up" oneself such that one is overdressed in the process.[42] A caution, then, is whether Christianity is best suited as a theological system or as grace-filled (albeit frumpy sometimes) insights about God's evolving relationships with us. Admittedly, there are problems with the Hebrew Scriptures and Paul, but for me as a Christian, the cross and empty tomb are God's invitation ever to see the particular against the whole—the entirety of God's ongoing story of salvation so that one does not get flummoxed by occasional incongruities.

SUGGESTED EXERCISES AND DISCUSSION TOPICS

Exercise: Understanding My View of the Church

1. Think about the relationships that have been liberating, formative, and affirmative: the relationships that have shaped you. List the characteristics of those relationships.
2. Think about different groups to which you belong. Then create a list of the characteristics of relationships of those groups.
3. Compare the two different lists and reflect on what makes a relationship liberating and formative. Have these relationships influenced your ecclesiology?

Suggested Discussion Topics

1. What is your ecclesiology and that of your church?
2. Does your church's ecclesiology promote community building?
3. Think about the Body of Christ as discussed in this chapter. Does it present challenges for your ecclesiology? How about hopes and dreams for the future—what are they?

PART 2

A PEDAGOGY
OF COMMUNAL FAITH

Chapter 4

A Pedagogy for Communal Faith

Ministry as Pedagogy

A STORY FROM A MAINLINE CHURCH

During my first week as the minister at a new church, one that I henceforth will call the "Main Street Church," a visitor knocked on the parsonage door. A woman in her forties introduced herself as a member and asked to talk with the new minister. After introducing myself, I invited her into the living room. We sat down, and she told me that she chaired the education committee and had been the superintendent of the Sunday school; that is until the previous Sunday when she and the rest of our Sunday school teachers had resigned. "So," she summarily decreed, "you need to find a new teaching team during the next quarter . . . during the summer months."

The church profile that I had read only a couple of months before listed education as the Main Street Church's strongest area and its highest priority. In my meetings with the Staff/Pastor-Parish Relations

43

Committee, the committee members lauded their education program.[1] So, what had happened betwixt and between? To make a long story short, except for my ex-chairperson, all of the other teachers continued on one condition: that the new minister evaluate the church's educational ministries and develop a new approach. What looked to be perfect in print was a burden to maintain: these teachers and others in the congregation were overstretched by multiple and competing demands, ones that made teaching as rewarding as standing in Tantalus' pool—the branches were beautiful and the waters inviting, but no spiritual repast was attainable for leadership.

I have found this a well-worn drama in faith communities. As faithful long-term teachers "retire" or give up the ghost, clergy and laity often ask me for advice about how to attract new people. I have some ideas, ones that typically are based on local specifics, a few of which I shall discuss in Part 3. Too often, though, we look for salvation through programs and sidestep epistemology's spirited insight, one of success's attendant spirits. Epistemology (or what we think to be so and how we discuss it) is where I turn in this chapter, and I will use it to flesh out my response to the "everyone-has-resigned" declaration of my ex-chairperson. This frames a much bigger and more significant matter than simply staffing Sunday school teachers and recruiting more volunteers: It presents a philosophical befuddlement rooted in the religious community's compartmentalized approach to ministry, an approach that alienates explicitly and implicitly related areas of ministry from each other. Borrowing from the work of Donald W. Oliver, a communitarian educator, I submit that religious leadership can inspire teachers and students anew by developing a fuller philosophical repertoire, out of which arise novel methodologies, but I shall back into this by first saying something about the concerns of the Main Street Church.

WHY IS THIS HAPPENING?
WHAT IS GOING ON AT A DEEPER LEVEL?

To address the challenge that I faced during my first week at a new parish, I took a step that most educators would take: I did a needs assessment. A needs assessment is a way of knowing who people are and where they are in their faith formation at both personal and communal levels. As a newly appointed minister, it was important for me to get to know the congregation collectively and individually, and to flesh out their concerns, hopes, and dreams. Moreover, as an educator it was critical for me to know people's needs, learning styles, and compelling life and faith issues before introducing new ideas and programs. Although the church leadership planned multiple get-to-know-your-new-minister events, after the surprising visit by my now ex-education committee chairperson, I knew that I needed forthwith to figure out emotionally and spiritually what was going on so that I could begin cultivating an educational strategy.

As a way of doing this, I created an extensive visitation plan that allowed me to meet with most of my members and constituents, including youth and those who had not been active for a long time, within the first six months of my arrival. To make it easier for individuals to decline a visit, I asked two of the longtime members to contact each household for me. Thanks to their hard work and the openness and curiosity of the congregation, in a short time I was able to meet with almost 85 percent of the people on the membership roll. By and large, I visited most people in their homes; this environment provided good conversation starters as I asked about photos, artwork, flowers, or gardening.

Visiting people in their homes and listening to their stories is an *insertion moment*.[2] According to Joe Holland and Peter Henriot, S.J., there should be three pastoral occasions before creating and implementing new plans. First one observes—one inserts oneself in a setting. Holland and Henriot define the insertion moment as *locating*

> the *geography* of our pastoral responses in the lived experience of individuals and communities. One discerns what people are feeling, what they are undergoing, how they are responding—these are the experiences that constitute primary data. We gain access to these by inserting our approach close to the experiences of ordinary people.[3]

Geography, or what I later call "spiritual geography," is paramount for education to work. It is important for ministers and educators to be acquainted with people and their context and to do so as an observer rather than as a critic. Adults learn best when their learning is related to their own needs and experiences. Contemporary adults live with multiple competing demands at home, work, and society, so they rarely pay attention to analyses that appear to be unrelated to immediate needs and issues. Jane Vella, a prominent adult education scholar and practitioner, provides twelve principles of adult learning and lists *needs assessments* as the first principle of adult learning—adults learn best when their learning is grounded in their life experiences and their interests are engaged.[4] Thus I adopted this insertion methodology as a first step in needs assessment. I visited people in their homes and listened to their stories.

To hear about the perceived needs of the people and the community through this insertion process does not per se provide a teaching or pastoral plan for educators and ministers. Social analysis and theological evaluation are the next steps.[5] The purpose of social analysis is to understand the observed reality in its broader historical, cultural, political, economic, racial, and social contexts. In other words, by culling and analyzing consistent patterns and elements, ministers and educators can descry how particulars influence people's relationships, including their views of authority, gender, race, ethnicity, class, sexuality, religion, and so on. These analyses can then be evaluated against communities' biblical and theological perspectives, and their relationship (if any) to that of the larger faith tradition.

As I listened to my parishioners' stories, I identified interests, concerns, and gifts, which later served as a resource for organizational restructuring. I will talk more about this in Chapter 9; in what follows, I comment on three immediate impressions and analyses therefrom.

A COMPARTMENTALIZED APPROACH TO MINISTRY

Utilizing social analysis and theological reflection to understand my parishioners and the church in a deeper and broader context greatly helped me put the shocking visit of the education committee's chairperson into perspective. The incident suggested programmatic fragmentation, a compartmentalized approach to ministry deeply rooted in an individualism that hinders churches from providing newcomers with much more holistic programs than group therapy. The following three features of Christian education as understood by many of my parishioners confirmed this.

First, many of my members felt that the primary goal of church education is to teach children and youth the Bible, Christian values, and tradition, and that their venue is the Sunday school classroom. They summed up Christian education as the process by which knowledge, tradition, and practices of Christian faith are passed along to the next generations so that children can grow up to be good people. When I asked parishioners to share their own experiences of Christian education, their narratives immediately went back to their own childhood Sunday school experiences and youth group activities. No one volunteered adult Bible studies, book discussion groups, new member classes, educational gatherings of the United Methodist Women and United Methodist Men, or other events—ones that are explicitly aimed at the spiritual formation of adults—as Christian education.

The English word "education" comes from the Latin *e* (out) and *ducare* (to lead), "to lead out."[6] The root word for education tells us that education is to help people find a truth that is already within them. It is not just a teacher transmitting knowledge to the young, but, rather, it is helping learners, regardless of their age, to remember what they know and to critically reflect on this in their present life contexts; it is to develop something new for the future. In other words, a good education integrates the past, the present, and the future, and helps learners develop their own worldviews. It is an activity that involves people's whole being, including their immediate and larger life contexts.

Education as something solely intended for the young completely dismisses the all-encompassing scope of education and becomes an ideologically driven rant.[7] According to Donald W. Oliver, key to building community is "a move away from living 'in one's head.'"[8] Modern society, which rapidly changes from one technology through the next, demands its schools to raise efficient operatives. Although schooling ideally is one of many different forms of education, formal education has become "the social analogue to modern technology."[9] This approach to education as formal schooling suggests that education is primarily for the young, and its primary goal is to attain fluency with systems.

Many mainline Christians are ideologically kith and kin to the Main Street Church. Learning primarily happens in Sunday school classrooms, and education is for the young. Although most churches are eager to have more young people and imagine that they are children- or youth-friendly venues, if one looks at the typical Sunday morning agendum, churches tacitly say that children belong in classrooms while adults belong in worship.

A second prevailing view of Christian education that I culled was that learning happens mainly through studying a set of curriculum resources and that teaching is the province of a committee, generally made up of young or parent-aged adults. Thus there potentially is a gulf between a committee's doings and the rest of the church's life. Even though, for instance, the Christian tradition esteems a teacher (see, e.g., John 3:2), worship is not perceived as education, nor is fellowship. This may explain the popularity of children's sermons. Worship is a passive experience. One watches it and occasionally sings or bows one's head. These are adult "activities." The one nod to youngsters is a morality lesson whence kids are dismissed to a classroom so that they grow up clueless about liturgy.

During my needs assessment visits, I asked people how adult Christian education was currently pursued and to name their best learning experiences. People frequently mentioned Sunday school Bible studies. The minister was often praised as the best teacher. In other words, no one associated liturgies, sermons, music, or fellowship with Christian education. Although people form their identity as Christians and learn Christian values and behaviors through being a part of a community that embodies Christian values in its worship, fellowship, and service, most of my parishioners failed to see these venues as teaching moments. In fact, I have met only a handful of church leaders and clergy who pay careful attention to the educational merit of these occasions, or who approach, for instance, prayer and music as part of a holistic curriculum.

Pursuit of a set of curriculum resources in a classroom context keeps the church in spiritual burnout. Admittedly "to burn out" is a verb, but it also, sadly, is a noun; it's a state of being or an ontology. Churches narrowly define what education is so committees think small. For example, I have seen various committees of many mainline congregations engage in different and yet similarly focused projects without meaningful and useful collaboration between them. The education committee and Sunday school might choose a Heifer Project and teach young people about the importance of sharing, encouraging kids to save coins. The outreach committee engages in a different-yet-similar project, soliciting the congregation's finances. Then, come Advent, the worship committee designs a liturgy around the theme of sharing with the poor for which Mary, Joseph, and the infant Jesus are well suited, and the missions committee collects nonperishable food items for a local shelter; however, both youth and adults would learn much more from working collaboratively. The sad result is that teachers lose steam since their well-intended extracurricular work exacts much from them, responsibilities that the congregation could easily shepherd since the larger church is engaging haphazardly in these activities anyway.

A third feature of Christian education that I identified through my assessment and observation was a lack of concern about social transformation. In her book, *The Art of Teaching the Bible: A Practical Guide for Adults*,[10] Christine Eaton Blair categorizes four different goals of teaching the Bible: Conversion and Encounter of the Holy God with sinful humanity; Common Identity with Bible People; Justice/Faith in Action; Spiritual Growth into a Holy Life. Blair's four categories can also be used for Christian education. I identify them as instruction, socialization, social transformation, and personal growth.

Christian education needs to provide good instruction about Scripture and tradition, as well as nurturing environments in which people form their identity. Christian education should also help people grow in faith through spiritual formation and think theologically and critically lest the good news of yesteryear not make it into the twenty-first century. All of these are important elements of good education. However in many churches, the emphasis is on instruction and personal growth, as I pointed out in Chapter 1. Social transformation is rarely emphasized.

When I asked my parishioners and other mainline Christians what Christian education means to them, they overwhelmingly opined that it is to be a better church member, and to develop one's personal faith through prayer, Bible study, and charity. Notwithstanding charity, social transformation came to mind only if I mentioned it. When I asked about Christian responsibility for addressing injustice, many respondents immediately identified their charitable donations as examples of transformative work. In other words, education is oriented primarily toward self-transformation, so the world God came to save (John 3:16) is fleeting except financially.

In sum, these three features of the Main Street Church—education as the classroom, education as the province of a committee, education without transformative evangelism—is ideological truncated-ness. Personal identity stands apart from the communal, as does the local from the global. This is bad geography. Christian education is concerned with people's whole being, including their spirit, and should not stop at an early age; rather it should be a lifelong process. It is an activity much bigger than learning about Scripture and tradition in classrooms, and it is bigger than any one committee's imagination. Christian education seeks to lead one out to new and imaginative ways of being in relationship with God and others. The root meaning of education and Christian education challenges us as mainline Christians to think differently and broadly. We need to move to holistic ways of imagining and being the church.

"CRAFTING SPIRITUAL GEOGRAPHY":
TECHNICAL KNOWING AND ONTOLOGICAL
KNOWING FOR COMMUNAL MINISTRY

In Kafka's *The Trial*, K talks with the painter about the law. The painter observes, "We must distinguish between two things: what is written in the Law, and what I have discovered through personal experience; you must not confuse the two."[11] Although I am using broad strokes, K's comment sums up an aspect of modern-day Christian education. Too often we draw a line between good ideas and experience. Our challenge as Christian educators is to cultivate ways to talk about the inter-connections between these two realms. Think back to your high school geometry class. The teacher talked about an indefinitely small point. At first blush, the idea makes no sense. How can a point point to a place and be indefinitely small? However, once one posits the point and stops fussing about the point's ontology, one then has a foothold whence to scale the universe. Ironically, the point is really there, but it is not there at all.

As educators, we seek to couple great ideas and spirited debate with a cosmos yet to be charted, so that one can begin to imagine one's own world anew. This sounds fuzzy, I know, so let me give a concrete example. *Cosmic art*—that's what my husband adoringly calls it. In the summer of 2006, he took me to Washington, D.C. He used to work on Independence Avenue, not too far from the East Building of the National Gallery, with its *Untitled* by Alexander Calder front and center. The mobile is 76 feet long and weighs 920 pounds, so it not-so-subtly commands one's attention. One cannot help but notice the mobile, but the mobile is not all that one takes in. As it dances through the atrium's heavens, the angles, colors, and shapes point to and pirouette with I.M. Pei's corners, expanses, and glass, and the colors and voices of the East Building's host of artists. For Christian educators, we need to craft a mobile of ideas and spirituality. Cosmic art is another label for what I call "spiritual geography." The pedagogy of my congregation had three locations: the classroom; the committee that oversaw education; one's own spirituality. These are fine domains but are provincial and thus fall short of reckoning with a cosmically transformative gospel (e.g., John 3:17). Borrowing Donald W. Oliver's epistemology, my congregation wanted to manufacture faith "operatives," so it relied primarily on technical strategies, the result being programmatic fragmentation and spiritual anemia. Let me explain.

Donald W. Oliver talks about "technical knowing" and "ontological knowing" as two critical vantage points for educators. Or as Oliver writes:

> It is our thesis that healthy organisms, communities, societies must apprehend a universe/nature/culture that is balanced between these two qualities of knowing. The central quality of ontological knowing is one's feeling for tentative connection—the way in which a novel occasion is to relate, harmoniously or destructively—to the larger world. The salient sense of technical knowing is the resolution of problems that arise for the individual or the group so that it may adapt in order to enhance its own survival, convenience, or comfort. Ontological knowing accepts with equanimity inevitable changes inherent in the emergence of being (birth), concrescence (growth), satisfaction (maturity), and perishing as the way of the world. It understands the craving of being for relationship with other being, since, in the last analysis, all is one. Technical knowing only allows the individual to understand the world at all when the individual separates from it. Technical knowing sees survival of self and extensions of self as the purpose of existence.[12]

Oliver goes on to say, "An essential characteristic of an adequate or positive cosmology is the balance and complementarity with which it describes the logical or paradoxical polarities that define the human common-sense world;"[13] in other words, such a worldview is one that is drawn from the confluence of ontological knowing and technical knowing. This is a way to consciously make use of affect, mystery, imagination, reason, and fact in one's pedagogy.

This brings discussion full circle to the Main Street Church's parsonage during my first week there. The chairperson resigned. She was frustrated. The committee was frustrated. It looked to me to resuscitate the program. My goal, instead, was to let the program die and then to plant pumpkins on its grave.

Oliver talks about a local school exercise where youngsters were given five slips of paper charting a pumpkin seed's maturation.[14] The goal was to teach kids how to sequentially order temporal events. Step 1 was to plant a seed. Step 5 was the arrival of a pumpkin. Oliver instead advises us to give kids real pumpkin seeds and a plot of soil, from which kids firsthand would begin to learn the growing process and a whole lot more. Kids would learn about soil and what one must do to nurture a seed. Teachers and parents could thematically weave the fruit of the children's labors into a discussion about agriculture, economics,

Halloween, and Thanksgiving. In sum, temporal ordering should be a pedagogical by-the-way of "pumpkinhood."

So have the kids in your faith community make bread. Is it leavened or unleavened? Talk about it. Talk about fellowship. Potlucks are a sacrament for many churches, especially for Methodists. Why are they important and how are they like communion? Discussion can go in all sorts of directions, including commentary on agricultural society and changes as a result of the second industrial revolution, in addition to theology. One thus can pull all sorts of "teachers" into the "lesson plan"—from farmers to food producers to cashiers at the grocery store. Talk about art—is making different types of bread an art? How so? What great works of art depict images of fields, bread, feasts, etc.?

This is but one example. There is a whole range of possibilities between the ontological and the technical, whereby one makes study more interesting and more interactive. Learners thus are also more likely to retain what they have learned and to discover new applications for it. Moreover, the cast of players—teachers and committee members—is greatly enhanced, which results in spirited new insights, and it also builds individual esteem in those who never imagined themselves as having something important to share with the larger community.

An adequate approach to Christian education must provide balance and complementarity—a spiritual disposition akin to the Wesley brothers' coalescence of piety and reflection.[15] Another way to phrase cosmic art or spiritual geography or ontological and technical knowing is with Shel Silverstein's poetic line about *falling* "Up where the colors blend into the sounds."[16] The gist is to explore new directions and redirect spiritual energy so that fact, symbol, cognition, spirit, and heart are never strangers to one another.

The church should approach each aspect of its day-to-day life as a moment for spiritual involvement—for engagement, enrichment, and insight—as we lay to rest well-worn models and cultivate new relationships between ideas, the day-to-day, and one another. Whereas some local churches are bedeviled with rabbit warrens of ideas and programs, whose efficacy depend on the staying power of a committee, person, or constituency, a productive next step is to cultivate an appreciation for a large-picture, spiritual geography; to see all of church life as the curriculum; and to create "mobiles" that merge goals and energies that "fall up" and blend new creations into new sounds about God, mission, and being.

SUGGESTED EXERCISES AND DISCUSSION TOPICS

Exercise: Learning about Schooling and Education[17]

1. If you can, find Harry Chapin's song "Flowers Are Red."[18] Read the lyrics first, and then listen to the song.
2. Compare the first and the second teacher from the song. What are their views of education? How do they approach teaching and learning?
3. Does this song resonate with your experiences of education or schooling? What about Christian education that you have experienced?

Suggested Discussion Topics

1. Reflect on how Christian education is done in your congregation. Who is involved in it? For whom is it designed? Where do you situate learning? When does it happen? Is it leading your congregation to new vantage points? Where are you headed?
2. What would be the challenges and benefits of moving away from a schooling model to an education model for your congregation?
3. Discuss ways to assess your congregation's educational needs.

Chapter 5

A Curriculum for Communal Faith

Broadening the Lesson Plan

Several years ago while I was out of town for a conference, I looked for a church on Sunday morning so that I could attend worship. After reading through a local phone directory, I decided to visit the one and only open and welcoming church in town. The advertisement in the phone directory read: "The One and Only Open and Welcoming Congregation in Town! We welcome all persons into our church regardless of who they are and what they are." When I am away from home, I choose a place of worship cautiously, for I have learned that not every church is welcoming to a woman of color. Thus when I found an open and welcoming church in a Southern locale, one known for its conservative theological disposition, I was eager to worship there.

I arrived at the church ten minutes prior to worship. An usher greeted me and handed me a worship program. Despite my obvious status as a visitor and as the only Asian-American worshipper, no one approached me to let me know about the church. Moreover, when I was about to

55

seat myself on one of the back pews, I forthwith stopped because three ladies were shaking their heads at the same time, clearly telling me that the seat belonged to someone. About fifteen minutes after the service started, I saw two other ladies join them.

In the ad, in the worship program, and on the bulletin board that greeted me in the entryway, the church explicitly declared itself as a welcoming congregation; however, as I studied the church's regular and special program offerings and building schedules, one could hardly tell whether this church was open and welcoming. There were few visible signs that this church was actively engaged in LGBTQ and racial justice ministries, and the makeup of the worshippers showed almost no racial and ethnic members. Maybe the church does a lot of racial and sexual justice work, but it was not visible to an outsider. As a visitor, I could not help but think that the church's self-proclaimed identity as an open and welcoming congregation was public relations bromide.

I tell this story to introduce a new way to understand the meaning of curriculum, one that helps the mainline churches move to holistic ways of being the church. The above story appears to have nothing to do with the overall theme of education, but for an educator this experience frames three different types of curriculum: explicit, implicit, and null. Without saying a word, this church taught a great deal about who they really are and what they are about. Through their interactions (or non-interactions) with a visitor (implicit curriculum), and through their list of existing and non-existing programs (null curriculum), as well as in their identity statement (explicit curriculum), the church presented its perspective on Christian identity.

When they hear the word *curriculum*, many people tend to think of a series of textbooks used to teach children and youth at Sunday school. As I explained in the previous chapter, such a view of a curriculum is the province of institutional education; it is not that of education. Education is concerned with people's whole being, and thus it is so much more than solely learning about new information and traditions in classrooms. Similarly, Christian education seeks to help people to be in right relationship with God through Jesus Christ, and to incarnate that relationship in their lives, in addition to gaining biblical and theological knowledge at Sunday school. Thomas Groome, a prominent Christian religious education scholar, calls this an ontological activity as it involves people's *ontos*, their very being.[1] Groome argues that good Christian education includes knowing Jesus in a personal relationship through faith, but it accentuates this relationship with the pursuit of justice; that is, how one practices justice and mercy and love. Through informative, formative, and transformative activities, Christian education seeks to complement people's whole way of being in the world, including questions about who they are and how they live. If we take this aspect of Christian education seriously, our understanding of curriculum, including its scope and context, is broadened by necessity.

The word *curriculum* is derived from the Latin verb *currere*, meaning to run together.[2] In educational contexts, this connotes a course to be run. Conventionally, "a course to be run" is narrowly identified with printed textbooks and lesson plans and explicit educational activities by which an institution oversees a course of study. In his book *Educational Imagination*, Elliott W. Eisner, a noted curriculum theorist, introduces broadened concepts of curriculum and offers a comprehensive definition of curriculum from which the mainline churches will greatly benefit. Discussing the subject of curriculum in public educational contexts, Eisner says that each school offers students three different curricula: the explicit curriculum, one that is the actual content, consciously and intentionally presented as the teachings of the school; the implicit curriculum, one that, through its environment, includes the way teachers teach and interact with students; and the null curriculum, those ideas and subjects in educational programs that are withheld from students.[3] By leaving out options and alternatives, the school narrows students' perspectives and the range of their thoughts and action. Thus the explicit curriculum, which is often regarded as the entire curriculum, is only one facet of teaching. In fact, Eisner points out that the implicit and the null curricula might have more influence over students than does the explicit curriculum.[4]

Every spring I teach Introduction to Christian Education. This course is required for the Master of Divinity degree, so the size of the class is much bigger than that of other elective Christian education classes. The school registrar assigns a big enough classroom for thirty to forty students. The room typically has forty-plus desks and chairs lined up facing a white board in front of which a tall podium stands. Before each class my teaching assistants and I spend a chunk of time rearranging the room; for instance, arranging the chairs and desks in a big circle. We also remove the podium from the room. I do this tedious work every week to embody some of my pedagogical assumptions, namely: 1) the professor is not the only teacher from whom class members receive new information, for I also am looking for new insights from my students; 2) students are practice teachers with one another and with me; 3) more precisely, we study the subject matter not only through written texts but also through "living texts" such as students' wisdom, insights, life experiences, cultural backgrounds, and critical analysis. I thus practically highlight the importance of dialogical pedagogy: students' own reflections, reading, speaking, and writing about their ministerial contexts are integral to our pursuit.

Let us imagine for a moment that, after I share such assumptions, I do not embody them in our learning environment. Although I present myself as a nonauthoritarian teacher who respects students' opinions, imagine if students were not allowed to speak in the class: that there were no conversation opportunities for students. My students would think that the dialogical pedagogy I promote is just talk. Students may be encouraged to participate in class discussions and activities, but if the physical environment of the classroom hinders it, dialogical pedagogy is less effective. When goals, pedagogy, and physical environment are compatible with one another, students better understand dialogical pedagogy so that good ideas and good experiences, theory and praxis congeal.

To let students know my pedagogical assumptions is what Eisner calls an explicit curriculum. Although the explicit curriculum has been conventionally considered as the sole curriculum, it is part of a larger whole. I can lecture about dialogical pedagogy without rearranging the room and without facilitating student conversations among each other, me, and the authors. In so doing, students might have learned about the theoretical side of dialogical pedagogy, but not with firsthand knowledge. In course evaluations, many students praise embodied pedagogy and shared authority in learning and teaching as the course's strength. In other words, and as Eisner points out, students name implicit and null curricula as pluses.

Resonating with Eisner, Maria Harris makes a critical point for Christian religious education; to wit, "The curriculum is both more basic and more profound [than printed resources]. It is the entire course of the church's life, found in the fundamental forms of that life."[5] Since the explicit curriculum is only one part of a curriculum, religious educators need to broaden their concept of curriculum to include the implicit and null curricula and to place more emphasis on them. Or as Karen Tye opines in her comments about Eisner and Harris's findings:

> Without ever saying a word, we teach what it means to be a Christian by the way we design our churches, by the way we welcome or do not welcome people into those churches, by the way we relate to

each other as a church community, by who is allowed to speak and who isn't—the list could go on and on.[6]

In other words, the whole life of the congregation—the history and reality of a local church as influenced by the larger church and society—is the curriculum.

Harris and Tye's point was clearly shown in the beginning story that I shared. Admittedly, I have not frequented any of that open and affirming church's formal instructional contexts, such as Sunday school. Maybe at these events the church has explicitly and invitingly proclaimed the good news; notwithstanding that, it is obvious that members have not considered other venues of their life together as a faith community as a curriculum for inclusiveness, because when only one racial group leads worship, the church effectively teaches about its views of race and ethnic diversity. When a children's program happens during worship, the members teach implicitly that worship is only for adults and education is for kids. When members are indifferent to a visitor, inclusiveness is on holiday. In other words, without saying a word, the church teaches a great deal about Christianity and spiritual praxis. Christian religious education occurs not only in the context of formal instruction coupled with an explicit curriculum but also through the rest of its life with implicit and null curricula as attendant pedagogical spirits.

Regarding explicit, implicit, and null curricula of the church, Maria Harris particularly talks about five basic forms of ministry that the church has utilized from the get-go: "kerygma, proclaiming the word of Jesus' resurrection; didache, the activity of teaching; leiturgia, coming together to pray and to re-present Jesus in the breaking of the bread; koinonia or community; and diakonia, caring for those in need."[7] Again, the whole life of the church uses a wide-ranging pedagogy to flesh out its cosmology. Tye sums up Harris's helpful framework, commenting that

> education in discipleship occurs not only in the context of formal instruction in a church school classroom, but also in the midst of fellowship, whether we are gathered for a potluck supper or participating in a family camp. It occurs in the context of worship, whether it is a Sunday morning service or a devotion time during a committee meeting. Education takes place when we are proclaiming the gospel, whether it is giving testimony during a service or voting as a church to take a stand for justice on a particular issue. And we learn about being Christian through the context of service, whether

we are building a house for Habitat for Humanity or sponsoring a walk for hunger. In each of these contexts, education is taking place, and people are being formed in their faith.[8]

So everything we do as a church is a curriculum. Throughout my parish and teaching ministry, people repeatedly and compellingly make this point. For example, I had a parishioner who joined the church after attending a church fellowship group for parents with elementary school children. Raised by agnostic parents, this mother had never been at a church and had negative attitudes toward religious institutions. However, she started coming to Sunday worship services and eventually joined the church after she spent time in fellowship members' homes. She volunteered that, even though she did not understand Christian theology and doctrines well, she longed to be part of the community to which these church members belonged. In other words, her identity as a Christian was formed by interacting with Christians at fellowship gatherings instead of through formal Christian education. You probably also know people in your own congregation who do not come to church programs but are very dedicated members of your service projects, such as Habitat for Humanity, ecumenical food banks, or shelter services. These individuals have probably learned about being Christian through these ventures, in addition to formal instruction about Christianity and church life.

As we have seen, through our explicit, implicit, and null curricula, we educate and sometimes mis-educate people. The question we thus need to ask ourselves is how much attention do we give each curriculum? Were we to approach our ministry with educational consciousness, the way we live together as a faith community would be more cohesive, welcoming, and powerful since we would be viewed as a community that walks its talk. Were the church that I had visited to have educational awareness of its ministry and had it paid attention to its implicit and null curricula, it could have been a truly open and welcoming house of worship for a newcomer like me.

Paying attention to all three curricula and having educational awareness in our approaches to ministry are particularly important for communal ministry building, for they make it possible to engage young adults and members who do not participate in any formal educational events. Throughout the mainline, we see fewer young adults in local congregations. According to Robert Wuthnow, a prominent sociologist of religion, since the 1970s mainline churches have been steadily losing young adults.[9] Moreover, the proportion of younger adults who are unaffiliated with local churches has been increasing. Compared to a generation ago when one person in eleven was unaffiliated with the church, now it is one person in five. Moreover, the conventional expectation that young adults return to church when they start a family is no longer true. Today's young adults either are marrying late or do not marry, and this cultural trend has tremendous impact on church attendance; even many of the married young adult couples do not raise their children in the church.

Another aspect of this demographic trend is that many of the folks who still belong to churches do not attend frequently. For example, while 46 percent of church members in their early forties attend church weekly, only 29 percent of people in their twenties do. Among those who attend church weekly, only 14 percent of liberal young adults (i.e., those affiliated with the mainline) do.

The disjuncture between a church's explicit curriculum and implicit curriculum, and disappointment with a church's null curriculum, arguably are some of the major reasons why so few young adults are involved in the mainline church. In other words, they are not disinterested in religion and faith matters, but they find that the church does not practice what it preaches. According to Wuthnow, among the surveyed groups that talk about religion with friends, young adults rate highest even though this group sports higher percentages of those that are uninvolved with a church.[10] Ironically, young adults avoid the church while they seriously pursue spirituality. Thomas Beaudoin, a Generation X theologian and the author of *Virtual Faith: The Irreverent Spiritual Quest of Generation X,*[11] explains this phenomenon as follows: Young adults consider the church as an institution entrenched in and colluding with middle-class culture. Young adults look for authenticity, caring, trust, and transparency in leadership, but they do not think these qualities characterize the mainline church—they do not think that the church deals with the issues and questions that are part of their lives. In short, young adults think that the mainline church has a curriculum whose explicit, implicit, and null dimensions are incongruous.

Paying attention to the three dimensions of the curriculum is also important to provide educational opportunities to more people. Let us think about the number of adults who participate in one congregation's formal education programs. I am speaking anecdotally, but typically about ten to twenty percent of Sunday morning attendees participate in these programs. To attract others in the congregation, churches offer classes and discussion groups on various subjects throughout the week, but the reality is that few people participate in short-term special topic classes. My clergy colleagues often complain to me about the lack of participation in their church's well-planned education classes. One colleague prepared a class on Christian parenting for his congregation. This congregation has had several instances of teen pregnancy and/or domestic violence. He was particularly frustrated by the lack of response from his congregation. Parents and other laity asked that the class be developed; however, when the class began, only three grandparents, none of whom were related to an at-risk teen, showed up. Later when this minister asked the church leadership, parents, and others about their absence, laity responded that their time already had too many demands to accommodate another program.

The frustration that my colleague felt is shared by many other mainline clergy. Robert Kegan,[12] a constructive developmental psychologist and an educator, provides an important insight for us mainline clergy and laity. According to Kegan, through ongoing—evolutionary, in Kegan's phraseology—interaction with others and as a result of our physical/cognitive/cultural environments, human beings develop an authentic sense of who they are and construct their truth accordingly. Calling the stages of human maturity "order of consciousness," Kegan says that in adolescent or early childhood, most human beings attain to the "third order consciousness," during which time an individual's identity derives from association with significant others (e.g., parents, peer group, communities such as fraternities or sororities, clubs, unions, nations, churches) with whom the individual identifies. Through this third-order consciousness, which is the majority of any given society, individuals find a "homogeneous fabric of value and belief, a shared sense of how the world works and how we should live in it."[13] In other words, most of us live our life through reciprocal relationships with our "intimate" communities.

However, Kegan ventures that the multiple demands of contemporary life from work, home, parenting, and relationships put modern adults in a tough situation, for life sometimes demands that individuals move beyond a traditional community's values and beliefs. Individuals then are called on to create and maintain new paradigms to meet modern life's demands amid other competing, conflicting, and powerful alternatives. Kegan calls this new paradigm a fourth-order consciousness.[14] With this backdrop, the frustration of mainline clergy with laity's devil-may-care participation in church education programs can be understood as a disconnect between third- and fourth-order lifestyles.

Although many people search for nurturing spirituality and formation, why do we not review our worship service from an educational perspective, in addition to the rubrics of liturgy? Are our explicit, implicit, and null curricula consistent with each other, and are there ways to bridge the cosmological no-man's-land between, say, third and fourth orders? We can start by reviewing our church's worship curriculum as we ask the following questions: What theological message is our worship delivering to people? Do the hymns that we sing and prayers that we say resonate with what we say about who we are as a welcoming congregation? Are we welcoming, and, if not, who are we and what is reflected in our choice of leadership? Do our sermons address real issues that people deal with on a daily basis? Does our choir sing anthems only written by European male classical music composers, ones that implicitly promote male-centered Eurocentric theology and worldviews? Were we to sing inclusive-language spirituals, has our denomination or local church been in conversation with our African-American brothers and sisters about cultural (mis)appropriation? Do we use Bible versions that promote openness and welcome others? Does our physical environment express an inclusive worldview? What do the paintings in the hallway and program summations in the narthex say about us? Do we effectively welcome only a select few through our programming? Do the curricula reflected in worship resonate with other parts of our life as a faith community, such as our outreach and fellowship?

One can go on and on with similar questions about other areas of ministry. The point here is that we need to review our doings with an educator's eyes so that our sayings and doings are in sync, for, in Maria Harris's words, "The church does not *have* an educational program; it *is* an educational program."[15]

SUGGESTED EXERCISE AND DISCUSSION TOPICS

Exercise for Seminary Classroom Context

1. Check your school's mission statement and analyze its message.
2. Visit your school as though you are a prospective student. Look around the campus. Pay attention to the architecture of your buildings, paintings, pictures, banners, classroom arrangements, symbols, chapel settings, and so on. What do you notice? Write down your findings.

3. Compare what you have noticed with your mission statement. Are they saying the same thing? What are the explicit, implicit, and null curricula of your school?

Exercise for Congregational Settings

1. Enter your worship space as an observant newcomer. If you grew up in a different religious traditions or denominational background, reappropriate that worldview for a while.
2. Notice features that are very obvious to you—what do they say?
3. Who is present and who is missing from worship leadership, selected hymns, prayer lists, Scripture readings, and sermons?
4. Pay attention to bulletin boards throughout the church. What do they say about who you are as a nonmember?
5. Does your building create a welcoming atmosphere?

Suggested Discussion Topics

1. What are some of the characteristics of your church's explicit, implicit, and null curricula? Do they match one another?
2. What are your church's implicit and null curricula (ones that hinder young adults from being involved in the life of the church)?
3. How is the church addressing the educational needs of members who are not able to participate in its current programs?

Chapter 6

Pulling It Together

Pedagogical Steps for Communal Ministry

In the previous two chapters, I emphasized that for communal ministry to work, mainline churches need to rethink the meaning of education and curriculum. Specifically, I challenged the mainline church to reclaim the meaning of education beyond schooling. Education is about people's entire being regardless of their age; it is much bigger than formal instruction done in classroom contexts. Education is also much bigger than studying a set of curriculum resources. Education is the transmission of education, and it is the formation of a people for the transformation of society. It the province of the entire church, in addition to being the raison d'etre of the education committee and Sunday school. As Maria Harris observes, everything we do as a faith community is pedagogical, and the entire life of the church thus is a curriculum. Unless we consider her comment judiciously, communal ministry cannot be easily done. The question then is how to put our insights and discussions from the previous chapters into practice.

Several years ago, I developed a biblical-survey curriculum for a Sunday school at a suburban Bay Area mainline church that I attended. Although I was asked only to develop a curriculum for their Sunday school (that is, for their children and youth), the process and the developed curriculum became something for the entire congregation. There I discovered that our collective doings were naturals for communal ministry. Here are some of my findings, prefaced by a statement about our mission.

As an initial step toward curriculum development, a few parents and I took turns hosting cookouts at our individual homes during the summer months. The gathering was advertised as a summer hangout for children and adults, and each host family made great efforts to find a date that worked for most people. Since the event was advertised as a social gathering, those parents who were not active also came and got acquainted with other parents and even developed friendship and business relationships with one another. Over the three cookouts during the summer, we discussed in depth our hopes and dreams for our children, and our expectations of Christian education. As a result, we identified three major things for our church's educational mission: biblical literacy, intergenerational relationships, and socially responsible faith.

Regarding biblical literacy, we thought out loud about the following questions: What are the important stories that we as adults know? When did we first learn these stories? What compelled us to keep these biblical characters in mind? What biblical stories do we want the next generation to know? The fall term was then populated with stories from the Hebrew Bible. The spring term featured New Testament stories.

Each month featured a story such as the Exodus, Esther, different prophets, etc. Then the parents divided the class time into storytelling, arts and crafts, snack time, and worship periods. Each period was about fifteen minutes. The parents then assigned themselves to monthly tasks overseeing one of these areas. For example, one parent who was a carpenter helped the young people to build a Sukkoth during their study of the Exodus. Another parent recruited several volunteers from the congregation to organize a service project that happened every other month as a part of their effort to raise social justice consciousness among young people and adults. In other words, she or he would handle an activity or recruit others from the church to help. The result was a church-wide education program, and a very successful curriculum. I attribute the success to the church-wide ownership of the curriculum, which was filled with many creative ideas from the congregation. The curriculum prevented teachers from burning out and feeling ignored because of its structure and wide ownership.

The new curriculum, which was a communal and an intergenerational project, also involved congregation members other than parents and their recruiters. Each young person from preschool to high school was assigned a prayer partner among senior members. They were paired as ushers, communion servers, acolytes, and readers for worship services. The prayer partners were also invited to ongoing monthly cookouts and asked to provide inputs for the unfolding new curriculum. The parents of younger partners and the senior partners were encouraged to invite each other to their special events such as dinners and extracurricular activities, including sporting events, dances, and music recitals. This partnership was an excellent way to address a goal of the religious education of the church (namely, to forge intergenerational relation-ships), and thus we were able to lessen a feeling of social isolation between different age groups.

According to Linda Vogel, older adults have a different set of needs: coping needs, expressive needs, contribution needs, influence needs, and needs for transcendence.[1] They are seeking dignity and self-control as they cope with changing physical conditions and economic situations. Despite their weakening bodies, however, they seek opportunities and places to make contributions to society based on their lifelong experiences and wisdom. They also seek ways to interact with the younger people. My church's new curriculum, which involved many of the senior members, provided such opportunities and places for seniors to meet these needs. Particularly, the new curriculum actively welcomed ideas and contri-butions from senior members, and in turn, the entire education had ownership by the community and percolated with newish old ideas. To develop our own curriculum also generated excitement and energy throughout the entire congregation. Since the curriculum development process and the teaching and learning practices were communally done, the congregation, which heretofore knew about my pedagogical and communitarian theories primarily through discussion, experienced com-munal educational and ministerial practices firsthand. Even those who were hesitant to participate in church activities became involved in the life of the church through their children's formation process, and those who felt forgotten found ways back to active involvement. Through this process, I learned the following pedagogical steps for communal faith formation and ministry, which echo what I said in the previous chapters.

First, forget the conventional idea that education happens only in a classroom context. Try to look at every ministry context that you and your congregation are engaged in as a learning opportunity. It would be an interesting and helpful exercise were you to review the percentage of people in your congregation who participate in formal educational programs either regularly or periodically. My experience is that about ten to twenty percent of active members participate in church education programs. If your congregation is in a similar situation, you need to think about how to provide educational opportunities to the rest of your members. If folks have not shown up for your many good educational programs until now, it is unlikely that they will show up in the future. But rather than waiting for them to come, let education happen in less-structured settings. I review this approach in Chapter 8, and as discussed in Chapter 4, the word "education" presupposes a community. Leading out or drawing out assumes a relationship between one who leads and the other who is led, and this relationship is not predicated on a traditional classroom. To lead or draw someone out, one needs to know the multiple communities that one's student is a part of, so that the student can grow as a responsible member of his or her communities.

Second, remember that everything we do as a church teaches certain things about Christianity and our church. As Maria Harris says, the church does not have a curriculum, but is a curriculum. What does this mean for practices of communal faith formation and ministry? How do we approach worship, fellowship, service, and other activities of the church as curricular? For this to happen, a congregation needs to have a clear vision and direction for the future and for the coming year. As I will explain in depth in Chapter 9, a congregation's vision provides directions and long- and short-term goals. Each year, specific goals and programs should be developed toward this vision. Then each program area and administrative life of the church can make concerted efforts to achieve those goals and to embody the vision of the church. The same goal and vision are reinforced in many different ways since each program area ideally would implement different aspects of the goals and vision. From a pedagogical perspective, this approach is also based on a sound educational principle. As Jane Vella's twelve principles of adult learning emphasize, the repetition of facts, skills, and attitudes in diverse, engaging, and interesting ways is necessary for learning to happen.

Third, do not assume that you already know your congregants. For communal faith formation and ministry, the entire community should take ownership of the church's ministry. Your role as a leader is not only to get to know them personally but also to assess their needs on an ongoing basis and to identify their gifts, interests, and current and possible contributions that can benefit the life of the church. In other words, if you, for instance, were to create a data bank of your congregants, you could keep abreast of available talents and meet changing needs without much ado. Moreover, because of the nature of individualistic culture that we live in, even though many people share common interests and ideas, not all of them know about others' shared worldviews. Thus helping congregation members to be connected to one another will be an important role for a leader to play: creating safe learning environments and sound relationships among members is integral to both personal and communal transformation. As I observed at my church, parents who were hesitant to be a part of church activities later became change agents for the new curriculum, because good relationships were developed with other parents, and these created safe and confident environments for one and all.

Fourth, do not wait for people to come to educational programs, but bring your religious education to where people are and where community is and can be created. As I have emphasized over and over again, doing a needs assessment is fundamental for a good education. However, a needs assessment that does not include a thorough understanding of your participants' life circumstances and modes of learning is not effective. As I will explain in detail in Chapter 8 where I present what I call the Traveling Bible Study as an example of bringing education to people, no matter how good an education program may be, if the program is presented at a time and in a way that most people find burdensome, they will not come. Be bold and creative with your where and how in creating faith formation programs!

Fifth, create as many opportunities as you can for your people to be informed and involved in your various educational ministries. Folks do not need to be directly involved in teaching as teachers and leaders; instead let them be, for instance, mentors for young college students who are pursuing similar vocational paths or prayer partners for young children. The idea is that the more people invest of their time and interests in your educational programs, the more likely they are to take ownership of education and do their best to make it succeed. Do not forget that communal faith formation and ministry is possible only when the community owns it.

As I explained in the previous chapter, English's *curriculum* has its origins in Latin's infinitive "to run" (*currere*). Too often we determine beforehand the course of one's run. Depending on the age and sophistication of one's group, this sometimes makes sense. The problem, however, is that we sometimes so narrowly determine classroom outcomes that we consequentially nix new insight by effectively decreeing methodological provincialism. It is one thing to talk about the Exodus and the booths (*Sukkoth*). Years from now, my students may be able to recount her or his learning when interacting with a family member or friend who is Jewish. But the likelihood of her or his being able to call Sunday school to mind probably increases to the extent to which learners and teachers are able to cultivate fluency between their world and that of the Bible.

In *The Evolving Self*, Robert Kegan situates evolution as key to understanding how one makes sense of the world.[2] Integral to this quest is how one understands her or his personhood in relation to that of others.[3] In other words, one can assert truths as the goal of a curriculum. Those truths, however, are always shaped by the self-understanding of the learner, which is developed in relationship with those of others in a community. Otherwise one ends up with a truncated notion of salvation that references individual sins but not systemic ones, nor has it to do with personal morality, which sometimes people affectively delink from questions about the larger community. In the next section of the book, I will present examples of such communal ministry and formation.

SUGGESTED EXERCISE AND DISCUSSION TOPICS

Exercise: Learning about My Own Teaching and Learning Styles

1. Reflect for a moment on your best and worst learning experiences. What makes them good or not so good?
2. Take a multiple intelligences test to find out your stronger learning skills; see http://literacyworks.org/mi/assessment/findyourstrengths.html. What is your reaction to the test? Any surprises or affirmations?
3. We tend to teach the way we learn. Reflect on the result of your multiple intelligences test and your best and worst learning experiences. Also think about how you teach. How does your approach incorporate your weaker intelligences, which may be stronger ones for your parishioners?

Suggested Discussion Topics

1. Think about people who are directly and indirectly involved in your educational ministries. Can you tell if your educational ministries are church-wide efforts?
2. Does your church have some form of a "gifts and interests" inventory of your congregation? If not, what would be a realistic way to create one?
3. List all the activities that involve intergenerational and communal efforts in your church. Think out loud about ways to expand such activities to all parts of your church's ministry.

PART 3

THE PEDAGOGICAL PRAXIS
FOR COMMUNAL FAITH

Chapter 7

Bridging Personal to Biblical and Social Worlds

Communal Bible Study and Preaching

Several years ago, I observed a group of Korean women leading a campaign to reduce the use of chemical products (e.g., dishwashing soap) at their church. This campaign spread to the entire church and to other churches too; it originated in a Bible study on the book of Genesis, one initiated and led by this women's group. Even though it was a time when the Korean church did not have much awareness of environmental issues and eco-feminist discourse, the women began the campaign after experiencing different types of skin irritation that appeared to be caused by household chemical products. So these women laity decided to do something about it, and the Bible study was the inspiration.

At their gatherings, women asked one another questions related to the use of dishwashing soap: What had they used before the advent of chemical products? Had they experienced skin problems or other illnesses due to use of these products? What did they know about the ingredients in these chemical products? Their questions generated a lot of storytelling, laughter, and reflection on their lifestyles. In other words, even though the women did not have much professional knowledge about the products and pollution, by sharing their experiences with each other, they were able to gather knowledge and frame the issue.

The women who led the gathering introduced detailed information about different types of soap, including all the ins and outs of these products' manufacture. As they did so, women participants weighed in with personal experience. With all of the information available, they then reviewed what the manufacturers had told them. Who benefits from the product, and who benefits from information about the products? Were women harming the environment by using the products? How could they change the situation? By asking these critical questions, women were able to see their own intentional and unintentional contributions to environmental problems. Then they explored ways to reduce chemical products by finding organic products and by learning how to make organic dishwashing soaps. In other words, the group collectively made a decision to reduce the use of the soap, with the goal of not using chemical products at all in the future. Through their collective study and reflections, and through helping each other to make connections between their biblical insights and their lifestyles and between local and global contexts, they together generated new perspectives and action plans for themselves, their church, and the larger community.

I do not think these women had consciously planned and led their campaigns with communitarian pedagogies in mind. Notwithstanding that, the way they worked embodied a good example of communitarian pedagogy and ministry models that I have been writing about: their approach was communal, holistic, and ontological, and its promise reached beyond the four walls of a classroom. Personal and communal stories—the life experiences of those women—became resources for further theological and educational discourse. The women's evolving pedagogy included aspects of character formation, critical thinking, and social analysis. They developed a new appreciation for their cultural traditions and faith practices and coupled these with political action plans for social change.

Since then I have been thinking about how to help mainline students and clergy to craft holistic, communal, and ontological pedagogies as those Korean women did. What are some of the pedagogical processes that I can demonstrate? More specifically, is there a new way to teach and preach the Bible to mainline Christians so that they can overcome individualism and become a truly communal church that works for the well-being of everyone in God's household? Wrestling with these questions as a pastor, and teaching and researching communitarian biblical pedagogy, I have found that postcolonial biblical hermeneutics is extremely helpful. Postcolonial biblical interpretations conjoin critical thinking with multiethnic, multireligious, and multicultural voices, and thus challenge mainline Christians to reconsider their notions about community and to redraw the boundaries for God's reign. In the following sections, I briefly describe postcolonial biblical hermeneutical principles and share a 5Rs approach, a methodology that I adapted from Christine Eaton Blair's *The Art of Teaching the Bible: A Practical Guide for Adults*.[1] I conclude with a sermon that couples postcolonial biblical hermeneutics and Blair's 5Rs approach.

UNDERSTANDING POSTCOLONIAL BIBLICAL HERMENEUTICS

Postcolonial biblical critics use a multilayered biblical hermeneutic, one that emphasizes the demythologization of the biblical authority, the demystification of the use of the Bible, and the construction of new models of interpretation of the Bible.[2] Their approach attends to denied rights of those on the margins, and it challenges centralized power (henceforth: "the center") concurrently. For this, Fernando Segovia, a postcolonial New Testament scholar, argues that there are three different and equally important worlds that readers of the Bible should investigate and analyze concurrently when they read and interpret the Bible: the world of the text, the world of modernity, and the world of today, which correctly suggests that modernism is but one interpretation of the world.[3]

Readers should analyze the world of the Near East or of the Mediterranean Basin in which the Bible was written and edited. This was a world of colonial empires—those of Assyria, Babylon, Persia, Greece, and Rome. The political, economic, cultural, and religious dynamics between centralized power or authority and those without power heavily influenced the production of the Bible. Questions about culture, ideology, and power are sine qua non (*quibus*, really) for understanding the text. For example, in a study of the Exodus, it is crucial to analyze the power relationship between Israel and the nearby empires.

According to biblical archaeologists, the biblical depiction of the rise of early Israel (e.g., stories of the Patriarchs, Exodus, and Conquest) was recast by biblical authors to serve their ideology and historical-national convictions. Based on excavation and the survey of material culture, biblical archaeologists present several new perspectives on the origin of Israel.[4]

For instance, the formation and settlement of Israel was a gradual one starting in the sixteenth century BCE. Moreover, the confederating process was a regional phenomenon. Most settlers were indigenous nomads who sparsely inhabited "frontier zones" that were suitable for pasturage, such as the Transjordan Plateau, the Jordan Valley, the desert fringe, and the hill country. Although some of the settlers were from outside of the country, including the eastern desert and the coastal plain, the majority of the settlers were local nomads, ones who had a symbiotic relationship with the city dwellers in Canaan.[5] Thus, the biblical depiction of the origin of early Israel was largely a "mythical memory of a Golden age" produced by orthodox, nationalist reform parties during the Assyrian crisis in the brief reign of Josiah, late in Judah's history.[6]

Therefore it is crucial for biblical readers and teachers to ask and analyze the motivation for biblical authors to idealize the Exodus. What was Israel's political situation relative to Near Eastern powers? Why did the faithful choose an invasion story to express their visions and beliefs? By asking these questions, we can better understand the world of the text while also demythologizing and contextualizing what would appear to be the Bible's reverence for centralized power.[7] Otherwise later generations fail to grapple with the implications of the editors' intention whose purpose may have been political rather than theological.

In other words, by failing to ask these questions, biblical pedagogy can unwittingly spawn an ancient empire worldview and perpetuate the status quo, which is promulgation of ideology rather than hope. Hereto, and to prevent possible union of different marginalized groups within its territory, empires often use the tactic of pitting groups against each other so that they compete for recognition as the model citizen and thus, ironically, become obstacles to a genuine sense of multicultural community.

Alternatively, groups within the empire might see the political landscape as one of self-preservation so that the interests of other groups are seen as inimical to one's own. This again shows the danger of a hidden political agenda in a purportedly religious text. For example, Latin American liberation theology, Korean *Minjung* theology, and Black theology found hope and justice in the Exodus story. Through a liberation lens, they understood the Exodus as a story of liberation from an oppressive and unjust society, government, and foreign powers. However, these different liberation theologies failed to consider the power dynamic between the Near Eastern powers and Israel. As a result, Native Americans—those who lost their land to foreign invaders who espoused the Exodus story—became even more oppressed in their own land. Although all of these groups were victims of imperial power, some gained liberation while others lost it, and all of these groups claim the Bible as their source of inspiration or oppression.[8]

According to Segovia and other postcolonial biblical scholars, another important consideration is the world of modernity, which now dominates biblical readings and interpretations. They particularly urge readers to pay attention to the expansion of Western imperialism, which is one of modernism's attendant spirits.

From the early mercantile phase of European imperialism of the fifteenth century to the Western empire-building era of the nineteenth century, to the contemporary capitalist stage of high imperialism, Western imperialistic traditions and Christian missionary movements traveled hand in hand. Missionaries, who were protected by the empire, justified foreign domination as God's will. Relying on texts like the Exodus, many Christian missionaries entered and took the lands of non-Christian Asians, Africans, and Native Americans, either to convert them or to promote self-serving claims of superiority and election.[9] For example, most American Protestant missionaries, who came to Korea in the nineteenth century, identified American civic religion and its lifestyle with Christianity and taught Koreans to follow American ways of life as examples of Christian living. In short, the biblical text not only has its own historical world and environment but also "travels in the world and participates in history, continuing to write its story far beyond its original context and readers."[10] Thus a biblical teaching that aims to challenge the empire and expand the notion and boundaries of the community must analyze how the West reads and interprets the Bible and its socio-political-economic assumptions.

The third world that we should consider is that of today's readers. Segovia points out that the reality of imperialism and colonialism is never imposed or accepted passively. Admittedly, there are people who readily accept Western domination, but there also are those who rail against imperialism. By analyzing how contemporary readers engage with the Bible and interpretations, we place the Bible in the context of their life situations and investigate the dynamics of the center and margin among them and their boundaries of community. In short, in biblical pedagogy the analysis of the reality of the readers' world and their reactions is as important as the worldview(s) of the Bible's writers.

These postcolonial biblical interpretations demand a radical communitarianism. They require biblical teachers and readers to challenge the universalizing norms of Western/European models—those that present a limited worldview and boundaries of community. It also challenges readers to see the world beyond their own communities, asking them to reflect critically on whether biblical interpretations that one community finds just and liberating are liberating for other communities. Even if a particular interpretation seems to be just, if it is at the cost of others, that interpretation needs careful scrutiny. The empire does not want different communities to be united against it; as long as each community concentrates on its own interests alone, the empire does handsomely. In sum, the question is whether "my/our comfort is at the expense of somebody else's."[11] Or, as Musa Dube suggests, whether our community's interpretation brings liberating interdependence to all the communities involved, should be guiding questions for every community.[12]

EXPLORING THE AUTHORITY OF THE BIBLE: THE FIRST STEP OF BIBLE STUDY AND PREACHING

When I introduce postcolonial biblical hermeneutics to my students, some of them naturally puzzle over how to apply this approach in their faith communities. Postcolonial biblical hermeneutics is a critical perspective that the church must embrace if it is serious about justice; but how does one introduce this approach? Here I highlight the importance of weighing the authority of the Bible as the curtain-raiser for Bible study and preaching.

Through my experiences of teaching the Bible and preaching from a postcolonial perspective, I have learned that it is important to discuss different views of biblical authority from the get-go. In most mainline seminaries, biblical theology is taught with the assumption that the Bible has dialogical authority rather than absolute authority, but many Christians espouse the Bible's absolute authority. So when there is

no discussion about biblical authority and teachers and preachers frame
Scripture from a postcolonial perspective, it is inevitable that some laity
get consternated. In the classroom, for instance, I invite people to reflect
on their own views of biblical authority by asking them to share what
the Bible means to them. Then I discuss the absolute and dialogical
authority of the Bible as a prelude to the study of the selected text.

In her book, *The Revelatory Text: Interpreting the New Testament as Sacred
Scripture*, feminist theologian Sandra Schneiders points out that when the
term *authority* is used, it always involves two phases: a claim to be
addressed, and someone who must respond to it.[13] In other words,
authority presupposes certain relationships whether they be power-laden
or not. Differentiating unilateral and absolute authority from dialogical
and relative authority, Schneiders contends that unilateral and absolute
authority is coercive and demands obedience and assent from its
addressees. It imposes someone's will on someone else. For the one-
who-is-addressed to hear the claim means to recognize the absolute
necessity to carry out the other's command. Here only the one who
claims jurisdiction and, hence, authority has the power to make final
decisions.

Alternatively, dialogical and relative authority invites the addressee to
commitment and engagement. The authority invites respondents to
investigate the truthfulness and morality of claims before making any
commitments. Therefore, the validity of the claim is tested and evidences for the authority of claims are pursued. The validity of the claim
is not permanent because whenever new evidence is presented, the
credibility and authenticity of a claim can be overturned. Schneiders
argues that the authority of the Bible is a relative and dialogical one; it
calls for commitment and engagement rather than imposing obedience.
It does not use physical force or intimidation, but, rather, it arouses
reaction from the depth of one's being.

This means that the Bible has different meanings when it is addressed
to people living in different situations. Their culture, social class, political
situation, religious backgrounds, and life experiences provide different
tools to understand and interpret the Bible. The authority of the Bible
does not and cannot remain the same to one and all. The Bible invites
contemporary Christians to reinterpret it relative to modern-day realities.

After introducing the above dialogical view of biblical authority, I
highlight that the Bible is a sacred book not because of its infallibility,
but, rather, because of God's presence and life-giving messages for all
people, persons living in all sorts of different and challenging situations.

So the question we as learners of the Bible must ask is not whether the Bible is literally binding; rather how it is best to bring God's life-giving message to God's people in each culture, time, and place. As long as we insist on the absolute authority of the Bible, there is no room for overcoming individualism, which sadly hinders the church from building a truly inclusive community.

POSTCOLONIAL BIBLICAL INTERPRETATIONS AND TEACHING THE BIBLE IN LOCAL CHURCHES: THE NEXT STEP

How do we proceed with the above principles in a faith community setting? Is there a particular way?

I use a 5Rs approach. It is a methodology that I adapted from Christine Eaton Blair's work. I have extensively used this praxis in local churches and seminaries and advise the following steps: Readying the Ground, Remembering, Reflecting, Reinterpreting, and Re-Searching.

1. Readying the Ground

This is when participants and I get to know about one another, especially the socio-political-cultural-pedagogical-theological background that we bring to the study of the Bible. In other words, this is a process of creating a teaching and learning community together. Through telling and listening to each other's stories and views of the topic together, people develop a sense of who they are and what they are about. Without such a sense, it is hard for people to create a communal learning process, an ingredient that is essential to create a community.

For me as a teacher it is also a time to assess people's different views of the world, texts, and themes so that I can facilitate the learning process with appropriate information and methods integral to transformation. Every time I offer a new Bible study class, at the first session I usually ask people to share why they are interested in the topic or the book that we are about to study and what their expectations are of the class. For example, if we were studying Exodus in the current U.S. context, one dominated by media debate about immigration, I would ask people to share their own family history of immigration. Through this process, I would remind people that each of us is an immigrant (a.k.a. participants in building something new); that we bring multiple perspectives and backgrounds to the study. Moreover, given our presumed varying stories about family origin and immigration, we should not assume that everyone in the room reads Exodus in the same way. In sum, the purpose of this process is to help people become aware of their biases and to develop respect for varying viewpoints so that they can hear anew old stories and reconsider what it means to venture along the "road out" to someplace radically different.

2. Remembering

This is when the class delves into the text, passages, or the topic itself. The main focus is to invite people to share with one another what they know about the meaning of a particular text, passages, or theme that they study, and what and how their communities have taught about it. They then are asked, "How do they now understand the theme?" This process is especially important if the study is introducing a radically different interpretation such as a postcolonial one, instead of the traditional male-centered Western interpretations of Scripture. In a class on Exodus, I would ask people what they know about the meaning of the Exodus; what and how their church addresses it; and from the perspective of their current knowledge, how they would explain the current U.S. debate on immigration. I might also ask people to share a modern-day Exodus story. I then would explicitly turn to the current U.S. debate on immigration to see whether Moses and the Israelite saga have any relevance.

3. Reflecting

This is when people hear what and how others, including scholars, think about the topic and critically reflect on the ideological background of these views. By comparing views other than those they learned in the past, people are asked to reflect on the process by which their understanding developed. Whose ideology shapes these views? Who benefits from them? In other words, this process challenges people to critically examine their own and their community's ideology, and as one considers other possible interpretations, one compares one's own worldview with those of others.

For example, in the Exodus study class, I present different inter-pretations of the Exodus, such as traditional androcentric interpretations, feminist interpretations, and different liberation theological interpretations (e.g., African American, Korean *Minjung,*

Latin American, and Native American interpretations). Then I invite the participants of the class to reflect critically on these different views and to give their impressions. I also provide some of the historical background for these various interpretations, the role of traditional interpretations by Western scholarship, and how these have dominated theological discourse.

4. Reinterpreting

In this session, teachers and learners explore new ways to approach the issue. This is also when I introduce postcolonial interpretations, utilizing core principles of postcolonial biblical hermeneutics (e.g., the power dynamics between the Near Eastern Empires and Israel, the internal socio-political situations and policies, analyses of character constructions, and the history of interpretations of the text by different empires of the West). I also invite people to think critically of ways to apply new interpretations to their own contexts.

5. Re-Searching

Here participants explore different ways to implement new meanings and insights that they have gained. What does the reinterpretation of the story propose for contemporary Christians? What new messages do we as readers find in the story? Asking these questions, I invite participants to re-search and reflect on new meanings that have emerged from postcolonial interpretations of the text. Now theory and application meet up: How does one understand illegal immigration based on new interpretations of the Exodus? What actions (political, social, cultural, and religious) should we, as individuals and faith communities, take to respond to these issues?

BIBLE STUDY AND PREACHING: AN EXAMPLE

So how does one apply this methodology to Bible studies and preaching in local churches? The following is a "for instance," one that applies the 5Rs to first century and twenty-first century husbandry.

Blessed Be the Goats! Re-Searching the Story of Sheep and Goats[14]
Matthew 25:31-46

1. Readying the Ground

To create a space for sharing by the participants and to raise everyone's comfort level, I generally start by talking about my own life story in connection to the text to be studied. In the context of the sheep and goats story, I might use the following:

> Where I grew up in Korea, we do not have sheep. In fact, until early in my adulthood, I had never seen a sheep other than in a picture, either on TV or in the movies or maybe in bucolic calendar displays. In contrast, living and breathing goats were easily found as they were raised by many of my neighbors. In a developing country, which was Korea's situation in the 1960s and 1970s, goats provided much-needed protein for people. Although my family did not raise goats, my next-door neighbor, who was a poor Korean War veteran with four children and a sexton at my elementary school, had several of them. Since his daughter was a friend of mine, I often went over to their house and played with their goats. I thus learned as a youngster that goats are peaceful and useful animals. Unless I annoyed them by trying to ride them or held their horns as rambunctious children sometimes do, they were great fun. I treated goats as though they were pets, sort of like cats and dogs.
>
> For my poor neighbors, goats were practical godsends that provided nutrition for the family. For the poor in a developing country, sustenance, especially animal protein, was not readily had. Cow milk was not then available to most Koreans, and meat dishes were mostly served on special occasions such as holidays, birthdays, and ancestor veneration days. Moreover, bovine dairy products like cheese were not a major part of the Korean diet, so goat milk was an excellent and inexpensive source of protein.
>
> What about sheep, then? I don't have much to say about sheep since they were not around. Things that I know about sheep are not from firsthand experience; rather it is primarily from others' stories about them. For example, my late

mother-in-law, Margaret Elaine Archer, grew up on a farm in Ohio. She rolled her eyes when ministers likened Jesus to a shepherd, punctuated with a chestnut about the virtue of sheep-like Christians. Elaine opined that sheep had no merit when it comes to smarts. For instance, when sheep would come to a corner in the pasture's fence, they would stand there and "baa," waiting for her to free them by turning them about. She observed, "Sheep are clueless about the ease of backing up and turning themselves around."

In a Bible study context, after opening with my own sharing, I then invite participants to share their own, say, stories about sheep and goats or farming.

2. & 3. Remembering and Reflecting

Here I invite participants to share what they already know about Matthew's story of the sheep and goats. Here are my own recollections:

And so the quandary for me? While growing up in Korea, I learned that the church praised sheep as models for Christian discipleship. Goats, on the other hand . . . even though I adored goats, I was taught that they were bad.

As a young Christian, I did my best to be a sheep, the best one possible. Every morning at 5 a.m., I went to the early morning prayer service before I went to school. "A good sheep should pray loud and hard," I was told and so I did. I never missed the church, Sunday school, or youth group. Even when I was out of town, I went to church. I sang in the choir and volunteered as a Sunday school assistant. I read the Bible every day and repeatedly won Bible quizzes and verse memorization contests. I also participated in a prison ministry and helped with everything that my church needed. However, when I was a senior in high school, I suspected that something was not quite right. I was one of the most active church members and was nominated to be the president of our youth group by my peers; but my education minister told the youth group that I could not be president. As a girl, to be president was out of the question. Only a boy could be president. Sadly, even though I was the church's most active go-getter, as a girl, I was destined to be a goat.

Although heartbroken, as a sheep I obeyed the decree. I had an inkling of my call to ordained ministry as a thirteen-year-old, but I also believed that listening to my minister was good training for my future ministry. So when I had questions about church life and life in general, I was told to be a gentle sheep and to faithfully follow the lead of the shepherd, and I did.

However, I finally arrived at the realization that no matter what I did and how hard I tried and prayed, I was not to be a sheep. As a woman, there was no way for me to be a sheep. The gate was open only for men. The denomination in which I grew up told me that I could not pursue ordination. Since women were bigger sinners than men, women could be only lay ministers and assist male leaders. To answer the call to ordained ministry, I became a Korean Methodist after long discernment. However, not long after I found a new church home, I learned that unlike male clergy, female Korean Methodist ministers had to remain celibate, otherwise their ordination would be taken away and they could not serve a local parish. In my opinion, it was another way of keeping sheep in power.

So what is the merit in today's reading? Don't get me wrong: I do not sidestep the reading's plea for the followers of Christ to walk their talk by being friends and advocates for the marginalized and by working for justice and peace. Instead I ask, what if one is born as a goat instead of a sheep? Or what if one does everything one can do to be a sheep, but still finds oneself labeled as a goat? What if one's hard work to be a sheep is dismissed?

What if one is both a sheep and a goat? As an immigrant woman, one who speaks with a strong accent, I am treated as a goat every day. At the same time, as a clergy and a professor who can afford to have a middle-class lifestyle, I clearly live like a sheep . . . ?

In a Bible study context, I would explain in more detail how the text might be interpreted. For instance, I would note that a traditional emphasis extols Christian charity and good deeds, and that alternative liberation interpretations highlight justice and equity for the marginalized as Christian responsibilities.

4. Reinterpreting

In what follows, I explicitly introduce a postcolonial interpretation of the text:

> One cannot help but ask whether today's reading really means what it literally says. I reread the text and ask several fundamental questions from a postcolonial theological perspective: What is the context for the reading, especially its colonial context? As we well know, first-century Palestine was under the control of the Roman Empire. So how did the Roman imperial policy influence the birth and growth of the early church and the writing of the gospel? Whose agendum is played out here, and for what purposes? According to postcolonial biblical scholars, the Gospel of Matthew is written by a community that bowed to Roman imperial policy as a survival strategy. In the Roman Empire, Judaism had relatively high religious freedom compared to that of other conquered nations and groups. The Romans allowed Jews to worship their monotheistic God rather than Roman state-decreed divines. Jewish religious holidays and rituals were observed in synagogues. In other words, early Christians who were converted from Judaism also had religious freedom as long as they were a part of Judaism.
>
> However, the year 70 CE brought catastrophic changes to both Jews and Jewish Christians. When Rome marched into Jerusalem and destroyed the Temple, it meant that Jerusalem and its doings, including religious affairs, were now under absolute foreign sovereignty. So the Jewish community reinvented itself. One of the unfortunate results was antagonism between Jewish Christians and synagogue leaders, ultimately resulting in a break between them.[15] In this situation, Jewish Christians developed resentment toward their Jewish kin, which unfortunately led to anti-Semitic sentiments and actions in the later church.
>
> In this context, Christians, including Jewish Christians, had to come up with survival strategies. First, internally, the church taught its members not to do anything that could bring Roman attention to them. Second, externally, the church endorsed the Roman Empire's hegemony. Both of these positions were reflected in many places in the Gospel of Matthew.

For example, in Matthew 18:15–20, we read the church's teaching on how disputes are to be resolved among members: "If your brother sins against you, go and show him his fault, just between the two of you. If he listens to you, you have won your brother over. But if he will not listen, take one or two others along, so that every matter may be established by the testimony of two or three witnesses. If he refuses to listen to them, tell it to the church; and if he refuses to listen even to the church, treat him as you would a pagan or a tax collector."

The court of final appeal in Matthew's reckoning is the church. The problem, though, is that I find it hard to believe that Jesus really said what Matthew *says* that Jesus said. For the shocking problem is that the church did not exist during Jesus' first-century perambulating, yet here Jesus is giving advice about it . . . ?

A good example for the external policy of Matthew's community is found in Matthew 28, especially verses 18–20, in which Jesus gives the Great Commission: "All authority in heaven and on earth has been given to me. Go therefore and make disciples of all nations, baptizing them in the name of the Father and of the Son and of the Holy Spirit, and teaching them to obey everything that I have commanded you." The problem here is mathematical. Jesus sends everyone along with a Trinitarian blessing, and yet Pentecost has not happened. According to Musa Dube, a postcolonial New Testament scholar, this Great Commission dovetails with Rome's empire expansion policy. Dube says that after the temple was destroyed, the Jewish people were struggling to maintain their cultural boundaries against the intrusion of the Roman Empire. In contrast, Matthew's community took a collaborative stance. In other words, as a survival strategy, Matthew's and other Christian communities complied with imperialist agenda of the Roman Empire, and the Western Christian churches have continued to do so throughout history.

5. Re-Searching: The Story of the Sheep and Goats and Its New Messages

What does this reinterpretation of the sheep and goats story propose for contemporary Christians? What new messages can you find in the story?

These backgrounds challenge us to rethink today's reading, especially the identity of goats and sheep. So who do you think the goats and sheep are now? As the Jewish community and the emerging Christian community struggled to justify their existence, they probably developed unpleasant communication skills, calling each other goats, branding themselves as God's flock. Since sheep were more valuable than goats and were regarded as more useful animals at that time in that region, being sheep-like was esteemed. Matthew's community, therefore, was telling itself and its Jewish relatives that, eventually when Christ returns, the followers of Christ will be regarded as the Shepherd's sheep.

This unfortunately is a text that has fueled anti-Semitic worldviews, and it also demands that we redeem the vocation of goats. As people of faith, isn't it our calling to be with goats *and* to challenge the doings of sheep and a society that lauds conformity? If, on the other hand, we uncritically adopt the church's traditional use of this text, we not only endorse the status quo but also effectively tell the marginalized to roll over and be sheared by the powers-that-be.

This morning I brought a handmade coffee mug that, years ago, a Quaker gave my Methodist minister spouse. It has a picture of a goat on it. Can you imagine a minister receiving a mug with a goat on it? When that person gave it to him, she said, "I believe that in this universe, there is nothing that can separate us from the love of God, as Paul asserts in the eighth chapter of Romans. However, were there to be a real hell, I know that you would be there, defending goats as remarkable role models for God's reign."

Everyone benefits when we unashamedly fulfill our calling to be the best of that to which God has called us, whether it be as a sheep or as a goat. The Good News is that at creation, God looked across all the contexts that God had created and called them good. Let us ever live into that potential in Christ Jesus. Amen.

In a Bible study class, I would invite participants to share new insights that they got from the study. Then I would ask them to be in silence as they think about action plans for themselves and for the community—both local and global communities—as inspired by the study. As the

Holy Spirits leads, participants are invited to share their new resolutions with the class.

OUR FAITH, WORLD, AND COSMOS

The above is a helpful strategy to Bible studies and preaching, a major goal of which is to challenge mainline Christians to think broadly and more justly. Whether one uses the above-mentioned or different methods, a major purpose of biblical pedagogy should be to challenge the status quo, especially a modern-day individualism and colonialism that keep the mainline from being a truly inclusive church.

According to John 3:16, God loves the cosmos, a term reduced to "world" (and a sometimes smallish one) by English Bible translators in the seventeenth century; notwithstanding that, God's cosmos includes everyone, and as John 3:17 boldly asserts, God's sees promise everywhere.

SUGGESTED EXERCISE AND DISCUSSION TOPICS

Exercise: Different Ways to Read the Same Text

1. Jump ahead to footnote 8 in the next chapter. Study the story of the Good Samaritan (Luke 10:25–37) from three different perspectives: Traditional, Liberal, and Liberationist.
2. Compare and contrast different interpretations of the same text.

Suggested Discussion Topics

1. The 5Rs model is one way to bridge a reader's personal world to biblical worlds and to the larger social-political contexts of our time. Discuss the importance of using sermons and Bible studies to connect these worlds to build and promote a sense of community.
2. Traditional and liberal interpretations tend to focus on the individual implications of the Bible, whereas liberationist and postcolonial ones push readers to go beyond personal contexts and worldviews. Discuss ways that you can utilize seemingly radical hermeneutical lenses for the building of a just community and society.

Chapter 8

Communal Bible Study II

The Traveling Bible Study

EXPANDING THE BOUNDARIES OF COMMUNITY: CONNECTING FAITH AND LIFE

"I have never known how much commitment a layperson must make to be a faithful member of a local church!" said a clergy friend of mine. A few years ago he changed his ministry context from local churches to his denomination's headquarters, providing administrative supervision over a sizable program. He confesses that while he was a parish minister, he often wondered why his parishioners—those who praised his sermons—would not come to education programs that he taught. On the other hand, he had lived a lifestyle that many of his former parishioners knew firsthand; namely, hectic morning and evening commutes, intensive work for over nine hours each day, juggling a complicated family schedule and childcare. He thus could appreciate his parishioners' programmatic absence. He ventured that by the end of the day, many twenty-first-century disciples could not muster energy to go to a church study group. Although many would like to participate in church life with vim, contemporary life does not allow people to commit to anything beyond constant review of their schedules.

Many readers would sympathize with my friend. Maybe they postulate that the Bible study model of Chapter 7 assumes that people luxuriate horologically so that time for study at church is not an issue. You may also wonder whether there are other ways to approach Bible study and other education programs for contemporary Christians. Alternatively, I introduce a traveling Bible study (TBS), a Bible study model that I used at the Main Street Church. As the name says, TBS is a Bible study that does not meet at one fixed location (e.g., at a church), but, rather, it moves hither and yon, meeting at different participants' workplaces or homes. For a ten-week span, the participants gather each week at a particular time of the day (e.g., during lunch) to reflect communally on how to put their faith into action and to deepen their relationships through, for instance, thinking out loud about the Lord's Prayer. The purpose of this model is to provide people who experience learning cul-de-sacs in church education programs to get easier access to great ideas. Goal-wise, the gist is to apply theology to places beyond the church; to cultivate meaningful connections between people's study and daily life contexts, thus to expand the boundaries of community. This particular model was developed to address issues that I faced at the Main Street Church.

The Main Street Church was an active participant in a local ecumenical ministry: Over twenty churches collaborated to provide shelter, food, clothing, and job training to people in need. Notwithstanding the program's meritorious pursuit, several church leaders and I felt that our faith community needed to move toward social transformation. Charity is good, but were we to forgo its necessity by nipping it in the bud through homegrown spirituality, all the better. Leaders thus proposed that the Main Street Church join other ecumenical organizations to envisage corporate, systematic changes to obviate injustice and poverty.

Many council and other church members objected to this approach. From their perspective, the church needed to focus solely on spirituality. To collaborate, as proposed, with, for instance, an organization that campaigned for health-care programs for uninsured children would mire the church in secularism. These faithful insisted that the church's mission was to bring souls to God through Jesus Christ, while, on the other hand, advocates for secular collaboration asserted that the church should couple mission with responsiveness to need lest misfortune derail openness to salvation. Moreover, albeit arguably, challenging the status quo and its efficacy are compatible with Jesus' teaching. As these two parties' views were spiritually, theologically, and sociologically "oil and water," the local church's adjudicatory voted to postpone decision making to study the issue further so that consensus could be had.

The council had several meetings with the representatives of the ecumenical organization and studied its missions and work. I conjointly offered a series of sermons and a Bible study on the Lord's Prayer. I chose the Lord's Prayer as the text for two reasons: First, the prayer descries the world-to-come, in addition to this world. I thus could affirm both groups' worldviews. Second, the Lord's Prayer teaches a prayerful how-to, for it commands us to live a prayer-filled life. Forgiveness, trespasses and debts, temptations are pivots for Christian growth. How we get our heads around any of these issues says countless things about our relationship with God.

Making connections between people's learning and life issues is a fundamental principle of adult education. Adults learn best when the subject matter speaks to their own issues, so that they can make sense of their lives.[1] Jane Vella suggests the following twelve principles for adult learning, which clearly show the importance of "conversation" between study and life:

- *Needs assessment*: participation of the learners in naming what is to be learned.
- *Safety* in the environment and the process. We create a context for learning. That context can be made safe.
- *Sound relationships* between teacher and learner and among learners.
- *Sequence* of content and *reinforcement*.
- *Praxis*: action with reflection or learning by doing.
- *Respect for learners as decision makers.*
- *Ideas, feelings, and actions*: cognitive, affective, and psychomotor aspects of learning.
- *Immediacy* of the learning.
- *Clear roles and role development.*
- *Teamwork* and use of small groups.
- *Engagement* of the learners in what they are learning
- *Accountability*: how do they know they know?[2]

These twelve principles can be categorized into four core issues: 1) connection between subjects and participants' life issues; 2) respectful and safe environments both physically and emotionally; 3) good relationships among participants and between the teacher and participants; 4) adult learners as doers and thinkers.

Christine Eaton Blair, who explores adult learning in the context of biblical pedagogy, provides very similar principles to those of Vella's. Blair observes that adults learn best 1) when the learning environment feels safe and supportive through respect, community, collaboration, mentors or models, good organization; 2) when their interest is engaged through the challenge of cognitive dissonance, layers of reflection, openness to the unexpected; 3) when their learning is grounded in their experience by application to life situations here and now, being treated as knowers, having their needs met; 4) when they are self-directed by learning how to learn, having control over the learning process, and unlearning inaccurate knowledge and dysfunctional habits, engaging in self-evaluation; 5) when their education speaks to mind, heart, and soul through symbol and story, imagination, and ritual and action.[3] In sum, both Vella and Blair repeatedly highlight the importance of meeting the needs of adults who are grappling with life's complicated demands as educators guide them about how to live their faith in a complex world. For this they emphasize that adult learners themselves should be the subjects of their own learning, and their life experiences should be respected as important learning resources.

Norma Cook Everist and Susan Nachtigal, whose work influenced the TBS, suggest that connecting adult education with ministry in daily life is one way to be mindful of the relationship between doing and learning. They argue that every life experience of adults is an important resource for adult education, and many of these experiences draw the parishioners' rest-of-life (read: non-Sunday) world into direct relationship with their spirituality.[4] Then the question that pastors and adult educators should wrestle with, according to Everist and Nachtigal, is how to make these experiences accessible to one another and to adults' own cognitive and emotional reflections: How do we befriend those experiences when we are not gathered as the people of God because we are busy being the church in the world? How do we "do theology" through modern-day technology in sync with the social sciences, medicine, business, and the law?[5] In other words, the task of pastors and adult educators is to help adult participants develop theological reflection skills through which they can meaningfully puzzle over day-to-day life. As an example of this approach, Everist and Nachtigal initiated learning groups in many different parts of the country. These learning groups would meet at participants' workplaces for a tour, coupled with discussion about, "What is God creating here? What is God forgiving here? How is God shaping community here?"[6]

As described in Chapter 5, through intensive and ongoing needs assessments of the Main Street Church, I learned that the members of the church liked to socialize together, especially over meals during the week and on Sundays. The church also had more than one potluck dinner and community meals every month. Although the congregation was divided over joining a social-justice based ecumenical organization, meal gathering among members continued. In other words, fellowship (e.g., gathering for meals) was an important curriculum of the Main Street Church, so key for the TBS was to couple this strong curriculum of the church with the immediate and ongoing needs of the congregation and the larger community.

THE TRAVELING BIBLE STUDY: A PROCESS

Although the TBS is a very different model of Bible study, I still followed the 5Rs model that I introduced in Chapter 7, an approach that is designed to help mainline clergy and laity to think about community more broadly and justly: Readying the Ground, Remembering, Reflecting, Reinterpreting, and Re-Searching.

Readying the Ground

Like any other good educational programs, the TBS had a preparatory step. First, I recruited people who were either disinterested in or not able to participate in the church's education programs because their work or outside commitments made long-term participation problematic. I highlighted the short-term nature of the study, and I emphasized the fellowship side (implicit curriculum) of the program over its educational worth (explicit curriculum). The program introduction read as follows:

A Theology on Tap:

Would you like to get together with your friends from church for lunch during a weekday? Are you interested in showing your work-place to your friends who want to know more about what you do and where you work? Do you want to deepen your thoughts on how to put your faith into action? If any of these interest you, please join Pastor Lee over lunch break on every Tuesday or Thursday for ten weeks. The group will gather at one of the participant's workplaces for a tour, followed by lunch at a nearby restaurant (or you can bring your own lunch) as we think out loud about what God is calling us to do in our lives.

After active advertisement and recruitment, eighteen people, in addition to the faithful fifteen members of the ongoing Bible study class, signed up for this new Bible study. In other words, over one-third of Sunday attendees participated in the study. I divided those eighteen into two groups according to the proximity of their workplaces and assigned the regular Bible study members, who were mostly retirees, into two sessions so that both Tuesday and Thursday groups had balanced numbers of working and retired people. In addition to advertising, I also held informational sessions after Sunday worship services to answer questions about the study. By programmatically merging fellowship, which already was esteemed by church members, with treks into the community, I was able to utilize food and fellowship's good energy as we began to reimagine study, spirituality, and mission.

Remembering

To help participants and nonparticipants of the study to cultivate a biblical and theological understanding of the Lord's Prayer, I preached a series of sermons about the Lord's Prayer beforehand for four consecutive Sundays. The purpose was threefold: First, since the TBS is done at a member's workplace and at a nearby restaurant, it was not possible for me to provide detailed information during the study time. Second, since this particular study model is structured around participants' reflections on the prayer relative to the workplace, I used worship as the medium for exegesis and theology. Finally, through preaching I was able to establish a link, albeit loose, between the study participants and nonparticipants; to have one-third of Sunday worshippers be a part of the Bible study proved transformative for the congregation, and it was important for nonparticipants to feel connected with the study. Without such a connection, it is not easy to create a shared vision for the church.

The first sermon provided general biblical and theological background for the Lord's Prayer. Different interpretations of the prayer were introduced homiletically. This was to elicit memories (*Remembering*) about how one learned and understood the prayer. The focus was threefold: traditional, liberal, and liberationist analyses.[7] Among these, the liberationist interpretation, which emphasizes that the Lord's Prayer invites us to live what we say and to uphold the interplay between the eschatological and historical and the personal and social as integral to Christian faith, was utilized and advocated. The traditional interpretations tend to spiritualize the meaning of the prayer, and the liberal interpretation, which prevails among most mainline congregations, is more focused on individual over community and tends to spiritualize bread or to transmute *our* into *my*.[8] According to Leonardo Boff, a liberation theologian, "Give us this day our daily bread" means that we ask only for what we need for today rather than accumulating things. When we ask for our bread, we also acknowledge that we are members of a community that depends on each other because one's own welfare is intertwined with that of all of our sisters and brothers.[9]

The next three sermons had the following titles: Hallowing God's Name, God's Reign on Earth, and Forgiveness and Evil. Like the introductory sermon, each sermon introduced different interpretations and invited the congregation to critically reflect on their own views of the prayer. The message highlighted in each sermon would be summarized as follows:[10]

- The Lord's Prayer is kith and kin to a standard Jewish prayer grounded on the notion of Shalom. God intends for all people to live in peace and justice, love and freedom, wholeness and fullness of life. Creation has a God-given integrity.
- The Lord's Prayer is God's invitation to be God's partners thus to perfect God's reign on earth, which already has begun in Jesus Christ.
- The Lord's Prayer is a pedagogical gift and invites a response from Christians.
- The Lord's Prayer is God's invitation to radical inclusiveness and love, and freedom from personal and corporate sin.

Each sermon also had an open invitation to the TBS; namely, "How can we live this prayer in our daily lives? What does it mean to say this prayer in my life? We will think out loud about these questions together in our TBS. You are welcome to join us!"

Reflecting

These foci also served as guiding questions for the study itself. Each week the group met at the workplace of the host of the day or at her or his home if the host was a retired person. The working hosts would show off their workplace, explaining their particular responsibilities. After the tour, the group puzzled over two specific questions with the host: 1) *What is evil here that clashes with God's presence?* 2) *What temptation prevents me (the host) from living my faith?* These two questions nicely summed up the key purposes of the study; namely, to make connection between faith and life, and to widen the faith community's boundary, which evoked powerful sharing and theological reflections from the participants. Once these questions were posed, reflections continued over lunch and at other gatherings for months on end. The following is an example:

> **A firefighter**: When asked what was evil, he mentioned unnecessary deaths caused by greed.[11] In his fire district, there was a person who owned multiple apartment complexes and violated safety codes with seeming abandon. In one unit with code violations, two young children were killed. They were children of poor, working parents who had to work multiple shifts to make ends meet. One night due to an unexpected delay because of the parents' commute schedule, those kids were left home alone for about ten minutes. During those minutes, fire broke out and killed both kids. The firefighter repeated that were the building owner not greedy, those kids would still be alive. His sharing evoked powerful and shocking emotional reactions among members and opened up opportunities for them to think about how individual greed influences and can harm the social order.

> **An executive officer of a transnational company**: After showing us her luxurious office with a grand view, this member of the Bible study, who oversaw the work of over nine thousand people all over the world, was asked about evil and temptation in what seemed to be a great work environment. After a long pause, she talked about American corporate culture and her occasional resentment. When she had had a lower-ranked position, one of her supervisors secretly informed her of a plan to lay off many of her co-

workers. She was promised a promotion. Even though it was a high compliment, she found it hard to stomach the company's doings and almost quit her job. When she was promoted as promised, she told herself that she would never be a boss like her supervisor. Notwithstanding that, she found herself doing what she found objectionable and came to feel trapped by corporate expectations. To do her job, she said that she often had to put her "Christian identity under the carpet." Through her sharing, other members of the TBS thought out loud about the work world's two masters: Could one put one's Christianity ahead of shareholders interests?

A sales representative: A faithful Sunday morning participant, who was never able to participate in other activities of the church, was very excited about this Bible study. She was a divorced, single mother of two teenagers and worked as a sales representative of a luxurious designer-maker women's clothing store. When members of the Bible study looked around her store, all of us had jaw-dropping reactions to the prices of the clothing: A lot of clothes were priced over one thousand dollars, including almost three-thousand dollar suits. When asked about evil and temptation in the workplace, she named consumerism and materialism. As a single mother, each month she struggled to make ends meet, but her customers frequently paid more than her monthly income on one garment, nor did they show remorse about their lifestyle. Her sharing challenged others to critically examine their own use of money and collectively to reflect on what Jesus would say about our culture's worship of brand names.

An insurance broker: When asked to share his reflections about evil and temptation at his work, he said unhesitatingly that each day brought temptation to him. He knew that he needed to earn a certain amount of money each month. Although most of the time he was honest about each policy he sold, sometimes he was tempted not to say much about the fine print. His commentary evoked deep conversations about individual and communal accountability to one another, neighbors, society, and God.

An elderly retired member: This strong-willed member, who was taking care of her ill husband, had only an eighth grade education and never learned how to drive. With her husband's illness, she became homebound. Notwithstanding that, she managed to be one of the most active participants in the TBS. When asked whether she experienced evil and temptation, she shared a sad reality of working-class retirees. Despite Medicare and a private health insurance policy, each month she and her husband spent approximately nine hundred dollars of personal funds for medical expenses, so sometimes she had to make painful choices between groceries and medical bills. In the past when I made pastoral visits, I sometimes had seen the couple drinking canned nutrition supplement for lunch, so I now realized that they did it because of financial necessity. This couple's situation pushed the members of the Bible study to get interested in our health-care system and to realize that it sometimes is hard to keep spirituality and politics apart.

These are a few examples. Deep theological discernment was inspired by a broad assortment of perspectives and vocation (e.g., that of a school guidance counselor, an auto mechanic, a nurse, an administrative assistant, etc.). This kept discussion lively—ideas and energy percolated through the entire congregation. Until the TBS, members used to imagine themselves as Lone Rangers when it came to workplace problems, and thus they felt isolated. The study, however, allowed them to meet others struggling with ethical dilemmas, and it provided them with opportunities for deeper theological discernment and social analysis. When about one-third of a congregation's active participants experience radical changes in their worldviews and theology, it is inevitable that the congregation's self-understanding and commitment to Christ would be transformed.

Reinterpreting

Those reflections and transformation also created radically different attitudes toward Sunday worship and sermons. Through my sermons, I tried to provide theological, biblical, social, and pastoral interpretations on weekly reflections and experiences. The participants of the Bible study had great interest in learning more about theological analysis from my sermons so that they could deepen their discernment skills as an aid in interpreting their own life and world events. This inspired nonparticipants of the Bible study: their heightened curiosity led them to puzzle over the relationship between Christ's resurrection and their non-church doings.

In the months following the study, I continued to emphasize the import of thinking out loud about relationships between the biblical witness and our twenty-first-century doings; that is, to see personal stories and experiences in connection with larger biblical stories. Christian religious educator Thomas Groome calls such an approach *shared praxis*. He describes the process as *five movements*:

Movement 1	Naming/Expressing "Present Praxis"
Movement 2	Critical Reflection on Present Action
Movement 3	Making Accessible Christian Story and Vision
Movement 4	Dialectical Hermeneutic to Appropriate Christian Story/Vision to Participants' Stories and Visions
Movement 5	Decision/Response for Lived Christian Faith[12]

If the Reflecting part of the Bible study was helping the participants to name and reflect on their present action, the Reinterpreting was about challenging them to connect their story and vision with the Christian Story and Vision (Movements 3 and 4). By critically examining their own stories and experiences in light of the larger Christian story and vision, class members affirm, question, and sometimes judge as inadequate or sinful occasions in their own lives, and thus participants are encountered by God who invites them to live more faithfully as God's people in the world.[13]

This interplay between the biblical tradition and twenty-first century was linked to the pulpit. After visiting the sales representative, the one whose sharing challenged the Bible study to critically reflect on consumerism and materialism, for instance, I preached about Deuteronomy 14:28–29, a passage that requires God's people to be attentive to the marginalized of society as represented by orphans, resident aliens, and widows. I highlighted the interconnectedness of our lives across economic, racial, ethnic, and cultural boundaries, and ways to be in ministry to those who live in the margins. I offered examples of how our take-it-for-granted lifestyle as middle-class Americans sometimes spawns unintended injustice and suffering to our marginalized neighbors. Here I talked about my past ministry experiences with transnational textile factory workers in Korea. In sum, my focus was on how we as middle-class Americans could be attentive to the marginalized of society and what specific actions and lifestyles God calls us to enact as twenty-first-century disciples of Jesus Christ.

Re-Searching

The Re-Searching part was the TBS and worship services' postlude. Since the idea of the Bible study was to address the church's consternation about whether to support social justice-oriented ecumenical organizations, the next step linked this issue to our pedagogy. In short, the question was how best to conjoin the study to the larger church curriculum. Both the Bible study and post-study sermons emphasized the interdependence between our own personal and communal lives and the wider world, and therefore the question for the congregation was what that interdependence specifically entailed. This question and task was communally deliberated by the church's governing board, which made two decisions about faith and praxis; namely, that the church would join the new ecumenical council, and that the church would work to improve the status and well-being of children from low-income homes. Thus church members, especially those participants from the TBS, actively campaigned in a state-wide effort to provide all children with medical insurance.

As mentioned in Chapter 5, Robert Kegan argues that the multiple demands of contemporary life push modern adults to go beyond the traditional community's values, beliefs, and systems. Folks are called on to create and maintain new paradigms, which meet modern life's demands. But according to Kegan, most faith communities generate little inspiration for contemporaries because of their idolization of traditional paradigms. The way we structure educational programs for adults—the time, place, and methods—does not respond to an ever-changing landscape, nor are age-old worldviews adept when it comes to contemporary adults' demanding lifestyles. If we want to create an authentic sense of community, Christian religious educators need to broaden the traditional church's understanding of community so that it actively engages the workplace, public forum, and the internet while it thinks out loud about God and the cosmos that God redeemed in Jesus Christ.

SUGGESTED EXERCISE AND DISCUSSION TOPICS

Exercise: Pray the Lord's Prayer with a Specific Person, Community, or Concern in Mind.[14]

Our Father in heaven,
hallowed be your name *in Main Street Church today*.
Your kingdom come *in Main Street Church today*.
Your will be done *in Main Street Church today*,
on earth as in heaven.
Give *Main Street Church today* daily bread;
forgive *Main Street Church* its sins,
and lead *Main Street Church* to forgive those who sin against it.
Lead *Main Street Church* not into temptation,
but deliver *Main Street Church* from evil.
For yours is the kingdom, and the power,
and the glory in *Main Street Church*,
now and forever.
Amen.

Suggested Discussion Topics

1. Remember a transformative sermon or Bible study that you personally experienced. Why was it transformative for you? How was it personally connected to you, your concerns, and your community's concerns? What actions did that study motivate you to engage in?

2. Discuss ways that you and your faith communities bring transformative experiences to your congregation by connecting the personal and social.

Chapter 9

Creating Communal Sustainability

Communal Church Administration and Program Development

A COMMUNAL ADMINISTRATIVE SYSTEM: A BASIS FOR COMMUNITY

I was once invited to be a consultant of a local church, known as First Church, that wanted to improve its educational ministries. First Church tried to move away from a conventional Christian education model, i.e., children- and youth-centered education, to a more intergenerational and communal curriculum. As part of my work, I observed their educational activities, worship services, and different committee programs. I also conducted interviews and focus groups to analyze the needs of the congregation and reviewed the church's history and various demographic and geographical contexts. Through these processes, I found that First Church had been working hard to be a good neighborhood church that tried to respond to the wounds of the world with compassion and justice. Each program area was greatly focused on outreach work, and the church was involved in many service projects. However, I also found that their outreach ministries were redundant and thinly stretched and that there were not many collaborations between different program areas. For example, although it was a small congregation without much financial strength, like most other mainline churches, the church was doing four major outreach projects during the Christmas season: the worship committee was collecting items for women and children in a local battered women's shelter on each Sunday in Advent; the education committee launched a Heifer Project; the outreach committee was asking for volunteers and donations to cover a local homeless shelter and food pantry for the month of December; and the youth group was asking for monetary and toy donations for another shelter. There were many faithful members with enthusiasm, creativity, and commitment. That notwithstanding, during my conversations with different constituencies of the church I heard over and over again from many members that they felt stretched and burdened at times.

As I analyzed reasons for their burden, I noticed that First Church did not have an administrative system that could function as the coordinator and facilitator of different ministry areas, and thus it could not create the intergenerational and communal church that they wanted to be. Their governing system, the Administrative Council, was a monthly gathering of the chairs of each committee, and it was no more than an information sharing place of each program area about their current and future doings. In one of the meetings that I observed, each committee chair reported what they were going to do in coming months. Although many of the projects that each committee was about to launch were similar in their nature, there were hardly any discussions about collaborating or combining the projects so that they could be more effective with their limited resources as a small church. Most discussions and consultations at that meeting were involved with the church's personnel, finances, and maintenance matters, but not with different programs.

I do not think that the reason for the low level of concerted action is because of their insensitivity or competition, but because of the lack of awareness that the organizational structure could help or hinder their efforts to build a community. Each committee had a strong sense of community among its members and tried to expand its boundary to the larger society. However, the inter-committee relationships, through which a sense of community could be created and deepened within the church, were not strong. In other words, First Church was trying to build a community with a compartmentalized structure and system that, in fact, contradicted their efforts.

I do not think that the situation of First Church is a distinctive one. I have seen and known many other mainline churches in a similar situation. Many churches put great efforts into creating an authentic community but pay little attention to their administrative structures through which community can be built or hindered. Such churches remind me of Jesus' famous parable about putting new wine into old wineskins (Mark 2:22). If each program area's doings are contents of a communal curriculum, i.e., wine, the governing structure is a wineskin that delivers wine to a banquet table where a community is. As Jesus said, without having a container that is compatible with the contents, it is not easy to use the contents for their purpose. If a church wants to be a communal church, both their programs and structures should embody the sense of community. This is what Eliot Eisner and Maria Harris call "explicit and implicit curriculum," as discussed in Chapters 4 and 5. Even with good communal and outreach ministry programs (explicit curriculum), if the way a congregation is working is a fragmented, compartmentalized, and individualistic one (implicit curriculum), the power of the explicit curriculum will be limited and less transformative. Therefore, in addition to building excellent programs for communal ministry through worship services, educational ministries, fellowship, and service programs, each church needs to ask whether it also has a governing system that embodies a communal spirit, process, and structure.

As a conclusion of my consultation, I recommended that First Church consider two things: 1) restructuring their administrative structure and system, and 2) revisiting their mission statement through a re-visioning process. First, I suggested that they consider restructuring their governing system, including the time, place, and the mode of the Administrative Council and separate committee meetings. Second, prior to any restructuring, I emphasized that the church should revisit their current mission statement to examine whether it represents who they are and what they are about; whether it generates excitement about the church among members as it provides directions for the future.

When it was a cultural trend, First Church, like many other mainline churches and organizations, came up with a mission statement. Their mission statement, however, did not say much about who they were or what they were about, nor did it say anything about their vision to be a communal and just church. In reading it one could hardly know the congregation's core values and commitments, as it was a vague and generic statement. Moreover, according to long-time members, since the mission statement was created, there had been no church-wide meetings to discuss ways to implement the statement in the congregation's corporate life and committees' specific works. In other words, there was no visioning process to flesh out the mission statement to the wider community so that it was owned by the entire congregation of First Church. Therefore, as time passed, the mission statement was forgotten, with the exception of a letter-sized copy of it posted on a corner of the bulletin board in the fellowship hall. In sum, First Church's mission statement, governing structure, and direction for the future were independent from each other. Therefore, I cautioned them that without revisiting their mission statement, which was not compatible with their current and future vision, restructuring the church's administrative system would not be effective. The administrative structure and system should embody and promote their mission and vision. The communal church that they wanted to be could be achieved only when the members embraced and took ownership of their vision. If a church's vision is neither clear nor widely shared, it is difficult to ask the congregation to move toward it.

THE VISIONING PROCESS:
A WAY TO BUILD A COMMUNITY

According to Lovett Weems, Jr., a prominent congregational studies scholar, a *mission* is what Christians and churches exist to do, such as worshipping God and bearing witness to God's purposes for human-kind, while a *vision* is what God is calling us to do in the immediate future in a particular place during a given period of time (in the next year, next three years, or some other time period).[1] In other words, if a mission statement is a general and broad purpose statement of who we are and what we are about as a congregation, a vision statement is a statement of a specific action and direction for the general purpose.[2] A vision gives a congregation a picture of what is possible and provides meaning, direction, and life to its efforts. Thus, by developing and sharing a common vision, a congregation can be united and become a transformative agent. Weems emphasizes that sharing a common vision unites the congregation, energizes it, focuses priorities, becomes the

ultimate standard for it, raises its sights, and invites others to participate.[3] Weems's insights challenge mainline churches to critically
examine whether their mission statements say who they are, what they
are about, and whether they have a clear vision for the future.

How then can a congregation develop its vision? What are some ways
to translate a mission statement to a vision statement that is appropriate
for a congregation? What roles can ministers play in the process? How
can all of these processes serve for building a communal church? I
recommended what I call a "visioning process." It starts with re-visiting
a church's mission statement. As a congregation critically examines
whether their current mission statement reflects who they are and what
they are about, they may want to revise it—that is, if the congregation
finds it is out of sync with their current situation—or they may focus on
finding ways to live their mission in their community by developing
long- and short-term goals and projects. If the church does not have a
mission statement, it may choose to develop one through communal
reflection on its identity and to find ways to implement its mission
within and without the church. I call all of these actions "visioning
processes." Jackson Carroll's three tasks of leadership in assisting
congregational members to go through a visioning process provide
helpful insights: "1) helping the congregation gain a realistic understanding of its particular situation and circumstances; 2) assisting
members to develop a vision for their corporate life that is faithful to the
best understanding of God and God's purposes for the congregation in
this time and place; 3) helping them embody that vision in the
congregation's corporate life."[4] The first step is doing a needs assessment through which a congregation can have clarity about who they
really are and what they care about. Since Chapter 4 discussed doing
needs assessments in congregational contexts, here I will focus on the
next two steps; namely, the visioning process in a narrow sense and its
implementation in a congregation's life.

The visioning process—critically assessing the whereabouts of the
church through revisiting its mission or redefining its vision—can begin
with developing a congregation's own vision statement. Carroll emphasizes that having a vision is not the same as having a vision statement.
Although having a vision is more important than having a statement,
expressing a church's vision in a written form allows the members to
discuss, share, and refer to it, and thus it creates platforms for
community building as the vision is owned by the wider community.[5] Whether a congregation has a vision statement or carries out its

vision in its practices of ministry, having a visioning process as a congregation can help the congregation to imagine a realistic future, as the process helps them to reflect on their own identity and available resources for their ministry. It also helps them to assess the whereabouts of a congregation: where the congregation is headed or how particular program proposals fit into the congregation's overall sense of purpose.[6] A periodic assessment of a congregation's whereabouts is critical to being a healthy church, since

> A congregation may or may not be headed in the right direction at this time and place in its life, but it may not know that unless it is willing to take a look at itself and its current direction and to make whatever adjustments are indicated. Who are we? Where are we now? What do we really care about as a congregation? What is our reason for being?[7]

Carroll's list of the characteristics of a good vision statement provides a helpful guideline in terms of what to assess:

- The vision is *faithful to the congregation's best understanding of its religious heritage.*
- The vision statement is *oriented to the future.*
- The vision is *appropriate to this congregation.*
- The vision statement is *realistic* in terms of the congregation's social context.
- The vision statement *contains both judgment and promise,* good news and bad news.
- The vision is, in so far as is possible, *a shared image of the desired future.*
- The vision statement is *specific enough to provide direction for the congregation's life but broad enough to encompass multiple but complementary visions* important to groups within the congregation.[8]

Each of these characteristics in turn challenges a congregation to ask the following assessment questions as a part of their visioning process:

- Is our life as a congregation faithful to God's will as found in Scripture and Christian traditions?
- Is our mission focused on only present work or does it provide direction for the future that we are committed to as a congregation?

- Is our mission manageable with our resources? Does it reflect our congregation's culture?
- Are we aware of the areas and values that we need to improve for a better future?
- Are our mission and vision owned by the whole community or are they suggested by a few leaders without dialogical processes?
- Do the mission and vision reflect different needs and hopes within the congregation?

If a congregation seriously asks these and other deep questions that allow them to discern their identity, mission, and vision, they will be able to draw a more realistic picture of themselves and thus dream a dream that they can achieve. Moreover, the process itself, which involves a wider community than just a small leadership team, will help to create a sense of community among members and more transparent operating systems. The process can also help members of a congregation take more confidence in their corporate future and ownership of their mission, since they invested themselves in creating the vision.

A WAY OF VISIONING: AN EXAMPLE

If the visioning process described above has such merits, how can a congregation, especially one of small or medium size and without many financial or human resources, do it? Here I would like to share the case of the Main Street Church. The Main Street Church, as described throughout the book, was a small congregation with aging members and burned-out leaders. Like many other declining mainline churches, the Main Street Church had changed their administrative organization a few times in their recent history—i.e., in the twenty years before I arrived—as an effort to accommodate their declining congregation size, which could not fill existing committee slates and stop the decline itself. Though restructuring organizational systems according to the changing needs and capacity of the congregation is necessary, the Main Street Church did it without critical examinations of the congregation's identity and status or the wider community's involvement. The result was that the enthusiasm that the change brought did not last long. Moreover, the church had a mission statement, but it provided no guidance to the congregation. It was forgotten by most members and became one of those things that the church did once when other churches were doing it. In sum, not only did the members and building of the Main Street Church look tired, but also its mission and spirit needed help. When I arrived at the church as a new minister, some of the members were talking about changing the structure of the church again. The church desperately needed a new vision, renewed energy, and a sense of a community, and thus a visioning process seemed necessary.

The needs assessment, a fundamental and initial step of a visioning process, was done in two different ways: First, as described in Chapter 4, I as a minister collected a great deal of data about the church and the congregation through my visitations. Second, the church held monthly town hall meetings over a potluck luncheon on Sundays, which originally started as luncheon gatherings to get acquainted with their new minister. When I visited most of those on the membership roll, in addition to their personal stories, interests, concerns, and gifts, I asked each of them two questions: 1) What does the Main Street Church mean to you? 2) What do you want to see happening at the church? The first question was about assessing their views of the current status of the church, and the second was about their hopes, visions, and dreams for the church.

The collected data were recorded and categorized according to their different criteria: age, gender, the longevity of the membership, held leadership positions, race/ethnicity, economic and educational backgrounds, and program areas.[9] The data categorization is an important process, and it shows the "ecology" and culture of the church. The categorized data were later passed on to the mission/vision task force. In the meantime, during church announcement time, committee meetings, and church council meetings, I shared a summary of data collected up to that point for two reasons: first, to give them a realistic view of the church; second, to envision a hopeful future by mentioning positive input provided by many people who had appeared to be indifferent about their church's doings for a long time. The sharing of data and news about inactive members also resulted in another positive effect in that it helped to create a deeper sense of community among members. For many different reasons, and probably because of the nature of an individualistic culture, both active and inactive members had been hesitant to reach out to one another. However, my sharing of inactive members' whereabouts encouraged everyone to be reconnected with each other. Another benefit of the data collection through visitations was that I was able to identify people's interests and gifts, which gave the church opportunities to expand its leadership pool. In fact, several of those I identified later served as members of the mission/vision task force.

The monthly town hall meetings were led by a few church leaders who were motivated by my visitation report.[10] The first few town hall meetings were devoted to fellowship and to listening to the voices of different constituencies. Then the meetings gradually moved on to brainstorming the future of the church. To help the members be realistic about the resources of the church, and yet not to be pessimistic about the future, the town hall meeting leaders carefully planned the event. First, they invited members to imagine a positive future for the church, and then they asked members to write their dreams and hopes on papers posted on the walls of the fellowship hall. This "Naming Our Dreams" session was conducted in creative ways. All participants were grouped and regrouped several times in different sizes and makeups according to age, gender, generation, and church program areas. It was an effort to make sure all voices were heard. The second time the leaders invited the participants to imagine possible programs that could help to achieve their aforementioned dreams. Again those named programs were written on papers on the wall in the fellowship hall. At the third meeting the participants were invited to carefully read through the list of dreams and programs. Then they were asked to categorize them into four different groups: dreams and programs that were already living, dreams and programs they could achieve in the near future, dreams and programs that they could achieve later with more resources, and dreams that were good but unrealistic for them. When we did this, the participants were pleasantly surprised by the realistic and possible new future that they could achieve. This process generated a lot of excitement and enthusiasm about the church, which was a good achievement for the Main Street Church.

With congregational information and group discussions at hand, the next step for the visioning process was to form a task force to develop a new mission and vision statement with long- and short-term goals. The church's Administrative Council, which is the decision-making body, invited eight people to be on the task force: four from the church leadership team and four others identified from my visitations. The composition of the task force, which also included the minister, represented the makeup of the membership in terms of age, gender, and other demographics. With available data and discussion summaries, the task force was charged to work with some of the guiding questions that congregational studies scholars provided:

- What is currently so central to our congregation's life that it must continue if we are to be faithful as a congregation? What does it mean for us to be a church?

- Who are the groups of people, inside and outside the congregation, who will most likely be the beneficiaries of this congregation's ministries five years from now?
- What would we as a congregation need to be doing to meet their needs, assuming these activities are in keeping with our core theology and values?
- Assuming that all the various groups of people and their needs are important, can we nevertheless put them in any order of priority?
- As a member of one of these groups that will participate in and benefit from the congregation's ministries, what is it that I personally and passionately want our congregation to be and do five years from now?
- What factors in our current situation and projected trends (congregational and contextual) are most likely to facilitate the realization of our emerging congregational vision?
- What factors in our current situation and projected trends are most likely to hinder or block its realization?[11]

After working with these questions and the data and discussion summaries for four months, the task force came up with a revised mission statement and a new vision statement with short- and long-term goals and presented them to the Administrative Council. After a few revisions made by the Administrative Council, a complete set of statements was presented to the entire congregation through worship services, church newsletters, and another town hall meeting. After the congregation's approval, a dedication worship service was celebrated with enthusiasm.

EMBODYING THE VISION:
A COMMUNAL ADMINISTRATIVE SYSTEM

The last step of a visioning process, which is probably the most important step, is to embody or institutionalize the vision in the life of congregation—in its structure, processes, and programs.[12] According to Carroll, most nonfunctioning vision statements, ones that are not used by a congregation, "typically have failed either because they did not really express central values and beliefs of a majority of the members, or because, even if they did, the congregation failed to embody the vision in the 'stuff' of day-to-day congregational life."[13] In other words, even though the Main Street Church went through a community-wide process, according to the wisdom of congregational studies, until the church embodied and institutionalized its new mission and vision, the process would not be complete. For this, the Main Street Church tried two major things: dissemination and restructuring.

. To embody the new vision in every part of the life of the church, it is important for members to understand and take ownership of the vision. Without taking it to their hearts it is not easy for members to create processes and programs that reflect the vision. For this, on two consecutive Saturdays the Main Street Church held a church-wide retreat where the new mission and vision statements were explained and discussed in depth. The first Saturday was devoted to understanding the new vision, and the second Saturday was spent discussing ways in which the church could implement it in church processes and programs. For the second day of the retreat, the list of dreams and programs created in the town hall meetings was brought back. The participants who signed up for different program areas looked at the list and prioritized according to immediate, near-future, and long-term programs. Moreover, even after the retreat the new mission and vision statements were continually discussed in each Administrative Council and committee meeting. The focus was not only on new programs that embodied the vision but also on critical and communal reflections on our embodiment of the vision.

At the retreat and ongoing discussion meetings, a consensus emerged that the Main Street Church did not have a structure that could support and embody the new vision. The congregation wrestled with the following questions: Do we have a structure that can embody our new vision? Does our structure create community? Does our current organizational structure support the community that we want to be? The Administrative Council charged the vision task force to carry on work for the organizational restructuring, and below is the suggestion that was made, accepted, and implemented.

The Administrative Council and each committee would meet at the same time in the same place. As described in Chapter 8, the Main Street congregation loved to gather for fellowship over meals, to have children around them, and to pray together. Utilizing these elements, the task force proposed that the church have a potluck dinner once a month.

During dinner the Administrative Council, which is composed of each committee chair, would eat together, discuss the agenda, and consult with one another about possible ideas for cooperation. After the meal the children and youth would be in their own programs while adults were in their different committee meetings, which would meet at different tables in the same fellowship hall. By doing this, when and if different committees needed to talk to other committees, they could have a short joint meeting or consultation on-site. This mode of meeting also involved more people in conversations beyond the report of each committee chair at an Administrative Council meeting. This mode of meeting also served as an excellent venue for community building and as a place for the creation of new ideas. After the meeting, each committee would gather for dessert and share their new and ongoing projects with one another and have other opportunities to create possible collaborations. Since the congregation had a corporate prayer as one of their high priorities in their new vision, the meeting was concluded with a corporate prayer focusing on issues and projects discussed at the Administrative Council and each committee meeting.

I devoted the majority of this chapter, which is about communal systems and program development, to a visioning process. I hope that readers understand my logic. When a church's vision is not central to its members and is not created through a community-wide process, new organizational structure and programs may not mean much to them. When the process is not communal (implicit curriculum), the product has far less influence (explicit curriculum). Communal administrative systems and programs should embody communal process, hearts, and minds.

SUGGESTED EXERCISES AND DISCUSSION TOPICS

Exercise I: Analyzing Your Church's Mission/Vision Statement

- What are its core values?
- Does it provide direction to a positive future?
- How realistic and concrete is it?
- How faithful is it to the current state of the church?
- Is your vision a shared one?
- Does it have a congregation-wide ownership?
- What programs are attached to it?

- Is it inclusive?
- Does it define the community's boundaries?

Exercise II: Looking at Your Congregation's Organizational Chart

- Does your church have a structure that can embody your vision?
- Does your structure create community?
- Does your current organizational structure support the community that you want to be?

Suggested Discussion Topics

1. How compatible are your church's mission and vision statements, organizational structure, and programs with one another?
2. What available resources can you identify to address the incompatibility issue?
3. Is a visioning process a possibility for your congregation?

Chapter 10

Being a Good Neighbor

Creating an Interculturally Communal Church

A couple of years ago, my colleagues and I experienced serious, intense, painful, and yet important conversations about cultural misappropriation and race issues on campus. A group of LGBTQ students, whose self-understanding was that they were dedicated to the promotion of radical inclusiveness, led a chapel service. The words of the hymns sung at the service were dramatically changed to gender-inclusive language.

The inclusive-language hymn singing provoked heated debates about racism and cultural insensitivity. An association of African-American students raised serious concerns about inclusive language hymns, namely that they are an outright misappropriation of African-American cultures by the dominant white society. Many hymns sung at the service were spirituals. According to the African-American students, the objections are as follows: First, African-Americans are keenly aware of problematic language in some spirituals, but the reason why they sing the hymns as written is because the age-old words are a reminder of the past and its legacy of oppression, so whether spirituals should be changed to inclusive language hymns is arguably a matter that African-American communities should decide. Second, the worship organizers should have discussed the language of the spirituals with African-American communities before editing the hymns. By not doing this, worship organizers treated African-Americans as though they are cultural misfits, and thus the organizers ironically breathed new life into the cultural chauvinism of yesteryear's masters.

Spirited discussion about racism and cross-cultural sensitivity followed. The entire campus community was invited to acknowledge the reality of racism. This observance included a wall of mourning on which people could write their reflections about recent events. Although most comments were thoughtful, a few took me aback. For example, someone wrote, "Whenever there is a conversation on racism on this campus, only African-American voices are heard. Asians are invisible here."

In my opinion the above story shows the incapability of multiculturality[1] to promote social harmony and equality across different cultures and communities. Multiculturality as understood and practiced in the United States often is identified as the recognition of the existence of different cultures, and the inclusion of those cultures to mainline discourse. It is obviously a huge step forward compared to monoculturalism. However, as the above incident on my campus shows, multiculturalism based on inclusion creates hierarchical relationships between the dominant culture and a marginalized group and fails to create harmonious and equal dynamics across different cultural groups. In a sense, multiculturalism has become a tool to keep the status quo, which protects the interests of the dominant culture and its collaborators, and thus further marginalizes already marginalized groups.

According to my own analysis, observations, and experiences as a racial/ethnic minority woman minister and theologian, multiculturality is the dominant mode of engagement of most mainline churches. According to recent statistics, the growing churches in the United States are mainly racial/ethnic churches while the Anglo churches are declining. The majority of the racial/ethnic churches do not own buildings but rent spaces from the Anglo churches. Despite good intentions of both parties, I have seen all kinds of conflicts between the two groups due to cultural differences. Moreover, since we live in one of the most racially and culturally diverse countries in the world, even if our congregation does not share the facility with our neighbors or does not have members from different cultural contexts, it is necessary for the twenty-first-century churches to learn how to engage with our neighbors. In the following section, as an alternative to multiculturalism, I offer interculturalism and explore how it helps the mainline church build a communal church that is also an interculturally engaging church.

MOVING FROM MULTICULTURALITY TO INTERCULTARALITY

The aforementioned incident on my campus shows that each group deeply cared about its own culture. Each group reflected on theology from its socio-cultural perspective and spoke out on behalf of its experience. However, because there seemed to be no conversation across the communities, the unintended result was misunderstanding. The irony here is that each community has historically been marginalized and oppressed, yet they appear to be competing with each other rather than working together. Regarding this phenomenon, a prominent Asian-American theologian, Rita Nakashima Brock, in a private conversation with me, said that the current mode of multiculturalism assumes that there is one big circle with its center. Once the one main circle of the dominant culture is posited, each of the other groups forms small circles around the dominant culture's circle (see figure 1). Most of the time, small groups are only talking with the center, so they are not in conversation with any other small groups in their neighborhood. The result is that small circles compete with each other to be the privileged dialogue partner of the dominant culture's center.

This is what a Korean German philosopher, Hyondok Choe, describes as *multiculturality*.[2] The concept of the "multicultural" was introduced to recognize and explain problems of contemporary society where several different cultures exist as a result of migration and colonization. Compared to the monocultural model in which the dominant group of a society does not recognize the rights of minority cultures or the dominant culture discriminates against those who do not belong to the mainstream, multiculturality would appear to be a step forward. However, Choe argues that if we are really serious about the existence and rights of all, we need to explore ways to live together in peace and solidarity that accentuate the unique contributions of one and all, for "the concept of 'multicultural' society is helpless facing the situation of living in parallel (in ghettos, for example) and cannot develop a model for living together."[3]

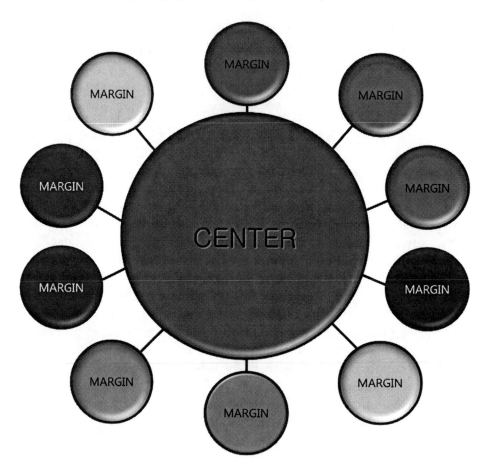

Figure 1: Multicultural Engagement

In mainline church contexts, I have seen countless examples of multiculturality that is not creating harmony among different groups. For example, when an Anglo congregation is sharing its facility with a racial/ethnic immigrant congregation, they have joint worship services twice a year on Pentecost and World Communion Sunday. On Pentecost Sunday, the minority congregation is invited to read the Scripture in their own language, and their choir sings an anthem. On World Communion Sunday, they are invited back to do the same thing and bring their ethnic bread to display on Communion Table and to share after worship services. Of course, this endeavor is better than nothing; however, I am not sure how such worship services help the parties to deepen their understanding of each other. Often those worship services become an entertainment of the host congregation by the "exotic" cultural congregation.

Multiculturality can sometimes even harm the relationship. For example, I know of a sizable congregation in a Silicon Valley that shares their big and beautiful facility with two different Pacific Islander congregations. However, the church has a policy that prohibits the two Pacific Islander congregations from bringing in food to the campus. Although the church is a local favorite place for weddings and banquets, and they host many social events for the community and the denominations, which also involve food, the church has a strong and restrictive policy regarding those two congregations and their food. Because of this, one of the Pacific Islander congregations, who eat together after Sunday afternoon worship service, holds their fellowship time at an off-campus location every Sunday. One year, two of their youth group members were killed by gun shots, and thus the congregation spent intensive time helping the rest of the youth group members cope with grief. Whenever the Pacific Islander youth group met on the church campus, however, the president of the board of the trustees of the Anglo congregation showed up to make sure that the youth group did not bring in any food to the campus. When the new senior minister of the Anglo congregation pointed out to his trustee members that the policy is problematic and racist, the board responded that the policy is a conventional practice of their own culture and that any congregation that wants to use their facility should follow their rules. As one can imagine, the relationship among three congregations is never equal and mutually reciprocal.

Kathleen Turpin, a Christian educator, specifies why it is hard for multiculturality to create social harmony and equality across different communities.[4] First, Turpin argues that it is because multiculturalism is currently misunderstood as inclusion of those at the margins. Although inclusion is much better than exclusion, the rhetoric of inclusion maintains the idea of a normative center and focuses on inviting others into its privileged realm. As an example, Turpin describes the following:

> A Korean pastor described a conference of his mainline Protestant denomination; the theme was "Who's at the Table?" and the purpose, to increase recognition of multicultural presence within the denomination. When my colleague was asked to share his perspective at the conference, he noted that, while he was at the table, he was clear that it was at someone else's invitation. He felt like a perennial guest in a place where others feel at home. He expressed hope that, rather than inviting people to a pre-established table, a new gathering place could be established that did not privilege one cultural starting place.[5]

This approach will always separate the mainline culture (the center) from other marginalized cultures and thus not be able to bring social harmony based on equality. Turpin insists that without dismantling the very idea of the center, multicultural efforts are only a means to keep the status quo.

As for the second reason for the incapability of multiculturalism, Turpin says that it is because people misunderstand that "a multicultural future is about 'having' enriching experience through encounters with 'the other.'"[6] Multicultural efforts are often led by the mainline culture as an effort to support the marginalized cultures' assimilation process. As a part of such efforts, encountering "the other" is necessary. However, since the "new" cultures of the other are very different from the mainline culture, they often come across as exotic objects of exploration of the mainline, which sometimes results in disrespect for the marginalized cultures. Turpin says that such interactions may enrich the dominant culture but not necessarily the marginalized, and the aforementioned example of a joint worship service is an example.

Third, related to the second reason, Turpin says that multicultural efforts that don't recognize hierarchical relationships among different cultures create false hope and perpetuate racism.[7] Without mentioning and dismantling cultural hierarchy, engaging in multicultural discourse as if every culture has equal rights is only a rhetoric.

The fourth reason is another misunderstanding that "a multicultural future is about a warm, uncomplicated community with people who are different from us."[8] Turpin insists that multicultural engagement means that people across cultural boundaries wrestle with real differences about important issues, addressing differences of power and privilege and struggling to hear one another when people speak in different languages and metaphors and express diverse values and ways of being. It is a messy process often involving conflicts. Without willingness to struggle and face problems and conflicts, engaging in multicultural efforts can only touch the surface. However, in reality, when conflicts arise, either multicultural engagement discontinues or the marginalized are blamed for conflicts.

The concept of multiculturality is also the dominant mode in current theological education. With increased interest in contextual theology, many theological educators pay attention to the issues raised by the marginalized communities and try to be attentive to different voices in their research and teaching. Problematizing the apolitical and ahistorical claims of Western universalism and the hegemonic notion that Eurocentric culture is superior to other cultures, contextual theologies are attentive to the long-silenced voices of the marginalized and reinterpret the Bible and church traditions through the prism of the social, political, economic, cultural, and religious contexts of people, especially those of the marginalized. Hereto, they challenge the ethnocentricity of Western theological views and highlight the option for the marginalized as the central focus of the Scriptures. However, it would appear that we theological educators are busy listening to and lifting up the silenced voices but are not paying much attention to creating new modes of communication among all these different voices. Brock ventures that communication seems to happen mainly between the dominant culture and a marginalized community, rather than among all of the communities. For example, as I mentioned in Chapter 7, Latin American, Korean Minjung, and Black African communities applaud the Exodus as the story of the God who favors and delivers the oppressed from injustice.[9] As the readers of these communities face oppression, they find hope and justice in the Exodus story, with its transition from slavery to liberation, themes with which these communities identify.

From Latin American contexts where the majority of the people had been colonized by Christians and continue to be oppressed by rich and powerful Christian leaders, liberation theologians George V. Pixley and Clodovis Boff celebrate the God of the Exodus who led Israel out of Egypt as a model for deliverance and liberation. Although God's love is universal, a love that would include even the Pharaoh, Pixley and Boff emphasize that in the Exodus, God's love is expressed as support for the slaves in Egypt: God heard the cries from the slaves and came down to set them free. Like Latin American interpretations, Minjung theology starts from the social, political, economic, and cultural contexts of the Minjung, the suffering people of Korea. They share the same view that God is the God of the oppressed. In Black African contexts where salvation is mainly understood as an event that one gets after this life, Jean-Marc Ela insists that the Exodus narrative invites Black Africans to reconsider God as a God of deliverance in this world. The Exodus invites them to enter into solidarity with people who are refused the dignity of being human, to denounce the abuses of established systems, and to intervene to protect the weak as did Moses.

In sum, above liberation theologies pay attention to the socio-cultural contexts, especially the unjust situations, of the people. They also invite readers to critically analyze their contexts, asking, why are things the way they are? Who benefits from them? Who is sacrificed and what needs to be challenged? Answering these questions, readers are challenged to reread the Scripture from the perspective of the analyzed contexts, thus to find new meanings from the text.

Despite their attentiveness to people's contexts and commitment to the fulfillment of social justice, the above liberation theological interpretations of the Exodus lead me to ask what light these interpretations shed on the incident on my campus. What does the God of Liberation mean for people who were at the margin in their homeland and find themselves at another margin in a foreign land, a promised land, like many recent immigrants? Do these interpretations promote harmony and peace among the groups in conflict on my campus and among diverse multicultural congregations in this country? Answers to these questions are even more complicated by the Native American interpretation of the Exodus.

Robert Allen Warrior, a Native American theologian, reads the Exodus as a Canaanite. Warrior says that the promised land of the former slaves of Egypt was the land of Canaan, and YHWH used the same power against the enslaving Egyptians to defeat the indigenous inhabitants of Canaan. The ancient-to-modern nexus? The God who came with the colonialists wiped out the Native Americans, the people who already lived in the promised land. However, across the sweep of theology, including liberation theology, the Canaanite side of the story typically has been overlooked. Although liberation theology empowers communities to read scriptural narratives for themselves and make their reading central to theology and political action, Warrior argues that liberation theology does so by ignoring the history behind the Exodus, and therefore it fails to differentiate between the liberating god and the god of conquest. If Christians are really serious about liberation and God's cosmic justice, the Canaanites should be placed at the center of Christian theological reflection and political action.

The Native American perspective on the Exodus is a noteworthy challenge to current contextual theology that works hard to lift up the silenced voices. Warrior challenges us to remember that the Exodus has at least two parts: deliverance and conquest. Each community's unique location affects how it reads the story and what it hears. Inattentiveness to all of the complexities of the past and present can easily lead to unintended consequences (e.g., the subjugation of other people). Failure to hear all of the voices can lead to acceptance of an interpretation that is lackluster, and other important critiques go unspoken. As a result, liberation pedagogy can unwittingly fall prey to its own uncritical ethnocentrism, over and against the Western universalism that it criticizes.

In sum, multiculturality creates a dialogue with the dominant group alone, instead of engaging all groups. Each cultural group proposes an alternative view to that of the dominant group. However, this dynamic often results in unhealthy relationships between the marginalized as they compete with each other to be a more important partner of the dominant group. This mode of engagement thus helps the dominant group keep the status quo, while putting other groups at odds with one another. However, if we are really serious about being a multicultural society, we should create a web of dialogue so that all of the groups are involved in multifaceted dialogue with each other, thus creating a just world for all (see figure 2). In this dialogical web no one group claims to hold the place at the center. I call such a dialogue an intercultural one whose goal is *liberating interdependence*.

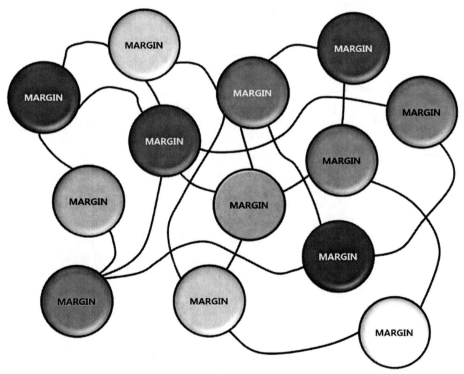

Figure 2: Intercultural Engagement

TOWARD INTERCULTURAL CHURCH
FOR LIBERATING INTERDEPENDENCE

The prefix "inter" in both interculturality and interdependence denotes relationship and dialogue between two or more different communities. Although they bring different perspectives and experiences to the dialogue, their relationship and rights are equal in principle.[10] About the nature of interculturality, the following description of liberating interdependence by Musa Dube, an African New Testament scholar from whom I borrow the term, is helpful.

Dube says that the term *interdependence* is used "to describe and to underline the interconnectedness of different histories, economic structures, and political structures as well as the relatedness of cultural texts, races, classes, and genders within specific and global contexts."[11] Dube continues:

> The postindependence experience of many Two-Thirds World countries has also rudely shown that "independence" from other nations and cultures, even from those that oppressed them, is neither practical nor the best means for survival. . . .
>
> The interdependence of nations, continents, genders, races, cultures, and political and economic systems, therefore, has always been a given and remains one of the most important aspects of survival. Nonetheless, most interconnections are built on foundations that are both oppressive and exploitative. The term *liberating interdependence* is therefore used here to define the interconnectedness of relationships that recognize and affirm the dignity of all things and people involved.[12]

To achieve liberating interdependence, which I consider the goal of intercultural dialogue, I insist that theological educators and ministers first need to ask whether our education and ministry bring the liberation of those who are the most marginalized among and beyond our community. When someone is suffering due to exclusion and oppression, while we are pursuing justice for our own community alone, no one will take our work for world transformation seriously. Therefore, while each community must work out its own critical norm of education and ministry, it is important that we as theological educators and ministers hold ourselves accountable to one another and test our community's norm in public discourse, in constant dialogue with those of other communities.[13] To test whether our pedagogy and ministry is creating liberating interdependence, we should ask an important question posed by Nami Kim, a Korean-American feminist theologian; that is, whether my/our comfort is gained at the cost of somebody else's.[14]

Second, theological educators and ministers would do well to remember that knowledge is produced by multiple interactions among different cultures and people, and thus we need to develop dynamic methodologies to frame such complexity.[15] In other words, to have liberating interdependence happen at all levels of our teaching and ministry, we should promote interaction among participants of different backgrounds and remain cognizant of the merits of interculturality. In the context of biblical hermeneutics, Kwok Pui-lan gives helpful commentary:

> We hear a plurality of voices speaking different social dialects from all sorts of backgrounds. We do not hear them directly, but through reported speech, which as Bakhtin says is "of speech within speech, utterance within utterance, and at the same time also speech about speech, utterance about utterance." We have to understand the dynamic interrelationship between the speech being reported and the speech doing the reporting. This requires us to pay attention to the relation between oral transmission and the written document of the Bible, the framing of discourse by the author, the multilevels of the dialogue, and the possibilities of reframing the retelling in the present situation.[16]

It is just not readers, but the text itself, who bring their various contexts to the text. The contents of our teaching and learning are also products of multiple interactions among different cultures and people. Therefore it is critical for us not to focus simply on the author's voice in the classroom or on the purported orthodoxy of church leaders. Instead we should investigate the ways different groups of people in Christian communities across history create meaning out of the text, using their different cultural backgrounds. We need to examine how these different interpretations create a multiplicity of meanings that interact with and condition one another.

For such investigations and analysis of the contents, I find post-colonial biblical hermeneutics explained in Chapter 7 extremely important and helpful. Especially in biblical pedagogy, it is essential to analyze how the West reads and interprets the Bible and to study the Bible's modern-day interpreters' socio-political-economic assumptions and their implications. Hereto, Dube, in commenting on Bible study, suggests the following questions for analysis and discussion:

1. Does this text have a clear stance against the political imperialism of its time?
2. Does this text encourage travel to distant and inhabited lands, and if so, how does it justify itself?
3. How does this text construct difference: Is there dialogue and mutual interdependence, or condemnation and replacement of all that is foreign?
4. Does this text employ gender representations to construct relationships of subordination and domination?[17]

By asking these questions, educators and ministers should examine whether we are integrating marginalized cultural traditions into mainstream views while accepting implicitly the existing paradigm. Alternatively, can we create liberating interdependence "in favor of living together *(convivencia)* with differences"?[18]

Third, for liberating interdependence to happen, the teaching process of theological education should be that of dialogue based on equality. Reapplying the phraseology of Elliott Eisner and Maria Harris, unless our teaching and learning process embody the said purpose of our pedagogy,[19] liberating interdependence will be less effective and may amount to pedagogical rhetoric.

Both interculturality and interdependence assume relationship and dialogue between two or more different communities who have equal standing and rights. In reality, however, these communities in dialogue are situated in various kinds of power constellations, depending on their race, ethnicity, gender, age, social positions, etc. In other words, not all communities are on equal footing. Therefore, challenging and analyzing the presently unequal interactions among different communities is an important part of pedagogy and ministry for liberating interdependence: What interests are represented worldwide? What types of values underlie the cultural interaction promoted by globalization? Who is obtaining the benefits of such interaction?[20] By asking these questions, pedagogy and ministry for liberating interdependence can help participants recognize the difference and diversity between and among one another, thus to examine critically their own privileges and ethnocentrism and to create a basis for developing new modes of dialogue and solidarity.[21] The goal of interaction and dialogue is not to explain perceived reality but to transform it. Herewith and in my own classroom teaching, I encourage and highlight the following:

To my white middle- and upper-middle-class students, who are the majority in my class, I issue a challenge to critically examine and study their own assumptions and worldviews as given form by white conventional cultures. With genuinely good intention, many of those with liberal and progressive theological views tend to think that they are sensitive to nonwhite communities and are doing justice work for other communities. However, as their Asian-American teacher, I find that many students fail to see that their culture and ethnicity confer special privileges on them. Therefore, I emphasize that they should try to understand what it means to be white before they try to understand nonwhite communities. Admittedly, there are sub-centers and margins (e.g., Appalachia) to the center (white culture in North America); however, in pedagogical discourse we typically "whitewash" the center as though it is not really there. White people need to raise questions about their identities and the privileges that they enjoy as white people. Often in intercultural conversations, those of us who are coming from nonwhite communities find it extremely difficult and frustrating to have serious conversations with our white colleagues because they do not seem to know much about their own cultures. To reflect on contributions that white persons can make to a community of liberating interdependence would be a good starting point. In a nutshell, talking about others without knowing oneself is nonsense.

To my students from the marginalized communities, I urge them to stop imagining nonexistent centers. There are many sub-centers, in addition to an imagined center; however, when we assert one norm, then we effectively limit our contributions to interdependence, as though our own thoughts are afterthoughts. Then, rather than inviting diverse groups of whites to the roundtable, we turn to our neighbors sitting around the edge and grumble about the "center," thus allowing it to control our actions and to define us. We need to reflect critically on who our conversation partners are and why we tend to talk to one imagined center rather than with one another and the plurality of "centers." Furthermore, we need to keep revisiting our goals—our hopes and our dreams—lest they be lost to hand-wringing about an imagined center.

What would intercultural dialogue look like in the classroom? Let me give an example. In my Introduction to Christian Education course, a course that about forty theological students take every spring, I try to help students create a community of liberating interdependence. To move beyond a multicultural pedagogy, I emphasize critical analysis of students' own social locations and assumptions and the development of skills for social analysis. Through the semester, students work in small groups on shared projects, ones that focus on learning and teaching a religious tradition other than their own. Foci have included Greek Orthodox, African-American, Asian-American, Hispanic, and Queer approaches to Christian religious education. In other words, through small-group work students are expected to learn religious education of the other whose rich and long-lived wisdom is not widely available in printed forms in the North American religious education field. After studying the traditions and practices of religious education of a different cultural group for a semester through participatory observation (including conversations with community members and reviewing available literature), each group presents what they have learned to the class.

About ninety percent of the students come from white middle-class Protestant backgrounds. Almost all of them identify their worldviews as liberal or radical and claim a commitment to social justice. However, from my Asian-American point of view, their approaches to social justice, especially race issues, are white American centered; e.g., they have a willingness to invite others to their privileged center, a multicultural approach. Since the class challenges students to be intercultural, it is unsurprising that there is struggle with or resistance to this methodology. Genuinely learning about and from the other requires my students to become aware of their own biases and assumptions, which can be a humbling experience. Notwithstanding this, every year I witness group presentations that include "coming out" stories, including students' realization of their own privileges and racism, intentional and unintentional ignorance of other traditions, and students' awareness of their resistance to genuine conversations with their neighbors. Frequently, students list the small-group work as the best learning experience of the class in their course evaluation. I do not intend to say that my students are completely transformed by my class and their small-group work within a semester. However, at least they learn that there are great traditions with which they need to be in conversation and from which they can learn. More importantly, I hope that they learn the critical necessity of interculturality for their ministry, and how to pursue it.

Another important benefit of this small-group work is that students learn how knowledge can be generated through a communal process. As they study their topic together, create a teaching program on the topic, and present their finding to their classmates, they have a firsthand experience of the importance of community in teaching and learning. They also learn ways to implement it in their own pastoral contexts. In other words, instead of having students solely learn theories and praxis in a classroom setting or having them learn theories in class and practice what they learn in their own context later, what I teach them in the class is immediately applied to their own presentation to their classmates. Below is my instruction for the group work in the course syllabus:

1. *Learning how to develop group dynamics/community building skills as a part of your educational ministries.* Community-less education is not a true education! As I will highlight in the class over and over again, and as you as a group will experience throughout the semester, knowing your participants (needs assessment) and building a sense of community are fundamental for good education. Before you jump into the work mode for presentation, please spend time to get to know each other in a safe place that you create together. As you get to know each other, your different interests, learning styles, and strengths will emerge, and then each member can contribute to the group's work in a unique and harmonious way.

2. *Reflecting on today's lesson and learning to be a teacher.* Each group member is expected to take turns to facilitate discussion: "What did you learn at school today?" "Why is it important for you?" "Why is it not important for you?" It is also the role of the facilitator to make sure that everybody participates; that no one monopolizes the conversation.

3. *Preparing for the group presentation that will be given at the end of the semester.* The group members are expected to share in the research and writing of the group presentation on a selected topic. Further guidelines for the group presentation will be provided by the instructor.

The goal of dialogue for liberating interdependence is not to persuade others through our opinions and thoughts but, rather, to transform reality through listening and being influenced by others, and changing ourselves. Both my African American students and LGBTQ students can be agents of transformation for each other through genuinely listening to each other and being checkmates for each other. Racial/ethnic immigrant congregations should not be regarded as objects of assimilation but agents of creating genuinely diverse church. For this the pedagogical process itself must be mindful of what it means to be liberating *and* interdependent. Otherwise, we repeat the same old patterns and look to be theological hamsters.

SUGGESTED EXERCISE AND DISCUSSION TOPICS

Exercise: Understanding Perceptions and Realities

1. Write each of the following words on its own note card: YELLOW, BLUE, ORANGE, BLACK, RED, GREEN, PURPLE. For each card, use ink in a different color from the name of the color on the card. For example, write the word YELLOW in blue ink. The word on each card should not match the color of ink in which it is written. Make as many cards—with as many different word/color combinations—as you can. (So, a second card with the word YELLOW on it might have the word written in purple ink instead of blue.)
2. First read the word on the card. Then read the color of each word.
3. Share your experiences about this activity. What does this activity say about our perception?

Suggested Discussion Topic

1. Discuss differences between multiculturalism and interculturalism. Is your ministry based on multiculturalism or interculturalism?
2. Who is the "neighbor" with whom your congregation needs to develop relationships? Is the relationship based on liberating interdependence? What privileges do you need to give up for the development of an equal relationship? What are the risks and benefits of such "giving up"?
3. Imagine and portray a truly authentic community based on liberating interdependence.

Notes

Preface

1. Maria Harris, *Fashion Me a People: Curriculum in the Church* (New York: Westminster/John Knox Press, 1989).

Chapter 1: Individualism, Collectivism, and Communalism

1. David Ng, ed., *People on the Way: Asian North Americans Discovering Christ, Culture, and Community* (Valley Forge, PA: Judson Press, 1996), 37.
2. Robert Wuthnow, *Sharing the Journey: Support Groups and America's New Quest for Community* (New York: Free Press, 1994), 48.
3. Among more than 1,000 interviewees of Wuthnow's research, the mainline Christians (United Methodists, Lutherans, Presbyterians, and Episcopalians, Congregationalists—UCC) occupy about 20% whereas Roman Catholics and conservative Protestants such as Southern Baptists and others occupy 21% and 59% respectively. Robert Wuthnow, ed., *"I Come Away Stronger": How Small Groups Are Shaping American Religion* (Grand Rapids: Wm. B. Eerdmans, 1994), 373-78.
4. Wuthnow, *Sharing the Journey*, 31–58.
5. Wuthnow, *"I Come Away Stronger,"* 350–52.
6. Wuthnow and his associates report numerous examples of this attitude of the majority of small-group members in their two books: *Sharing the Journey* and *"I Come Away Stronger."*
7. Wuthnow, *Sharing the Journey*, 193–94.
8. It is a common view in cultural psychology that Hofstede's book is the beginning of the study of individualism and communalism. See Cigdem Kagitcibasi

"A Critical Appraisal of Individualism and Collectivism: Toward a New Foundation," in *Individualism and Collectivism: Theory, Method, and Applications*, edited by Uichol Kim, Harry C. Triandis, Cigdem Kagitcibasi, Sang-Chin Choi, and Gene Yoon (Thousand Oaks: Sage Publications, 1994), 52; K. Leung and M. H. Bond, "The Impact of Cultural Collectivism on Reward Allocation," *Journal of Personality and Psychology* 47 (1984): 793–804.

9. Geert Hofstede, *Cultures and Organizations: Software of the Mind* (London: McGraw Hill, 1991), 51.

10. Harry C. Triandis, *Collectivism vs. Individualism: A Reconceptualization* (unpublished manuscript, University of Illinois), quoted in Seong-Yeul Han and Chang-Yil Ahn, "Collectivism and Individualism in Korea," in *Psychology of the Korean People: Collectivism and Individualism*, edited by Gene Yoon and Sang-Chin Choi (Seoul: Dong-A Publishing & Printing Co., 1994), 332.

11. Geert Hofstede, *Culture's Consequences: International Differences in Work-Related Values* (Newbury Park: Sage Press, 1980).

12. Ibid., 2.

13. C. H. Hui and Harry C. Triandis, "Individualism-Collectivism: A Study of Cross-Cultural Researchers," *Journal of Cross-Cultural Psychology* 17, no. 2 (1986): 225–48.

14. Harry C. Triandis, et al., "Individualism and Collectivism: Cross-Cultural Perspective on Self-Ingroup Relationship," *Journal of Personality and Social Psychology* 54 (1988): 335.

15. Soo-Won Lee, "The Cheong Space: A Zone of Non-exchange in Korean Human Relationships," in *Psychology of the Korean People*, edited by Yoon and Choi, 92–94.

16. Hazel R. Markus and Shinobu Kitayama, "Culture and the Self: Implications for Cognitions, Emotion, and Motivations," *Psychological Review* 98 (1991): 228.

17. I thank the Rev. Mitsuho Okado, a Japanese D.Min. graduate of Pacific School of Religion, for helping me understand the meaning of *jibun*.

18. Markus and Kitayama, "Culture and the Self": 224–53.

19. M. Brinton Lykes, "Gender and Individualistic vs. Collectivist Bases for Notions about the Self," *Journal of Personality* 53 (1985): 356; Harry C. Triandis, *Individualism and Collectivism: New Direction in Social Psychology* (Boulder: Westview Press, 1995), 43–105.

20. Robert Bellah, et al., *Habits of the Heart: Individualism and Commitment in American Life* (Berkeley, University of California Press, 1985), 7.

21. Triandis, *Individualism and Collectivism*, 61–72.

22. John Locke, *Second Treatise of Government*, edited by C. B. MacPherson (Indianapolis: Hackett Publishing Company, 1980), § 44.

23. M. Brinton Lykes, *Autonomous Individualism verses Social Individuality: Towards an Alternative Understanding of the Self* (Ph. D. dissertation, Boston College, 1984), 1.

24. Ibid., 17.

25. Edward Sampson, *Celebrating the Other: A Dialogic Account of Human Nature* (Boulder: Westview Press, 1993), 4.

26. Ibid., 72.

27. Ibid., 42–65; B. R. Slugoski and G. P. Ginsburg, "Ego Identity and Explanatory Research," in *Texts of Identity*, edited by John Shorter and Kenneth Gergen (Thousand Oaks: Sage, 1989), 36–55.

28. Sampson, *Celebrating the Other*, 4.

29. Ibid., 77–93.

30. Ibid., 138.

31. Kathryn P. Addelson, *Moral Passages: Toward a Collectivist Moral Theory* (New York: Routledge, 1994), xi.

32. Ibid., 168.

33. Sang-Chin Choi and Soo-Hyang Choi, "We-ness: A Korean Discourse of Collectivism," in *Psychology of the Korean People*, edited by Yoon and Choi, 57-84; Lykes, "Gender and Individualistic vs. Collectivist Bases for Notions about the Self."

34. Ibid., 57.

35. Ibid., 63.

36. Soo-Won Lee, "The Cheong Space: A Zone of Non-exchange in Korean Human Relationships," in *Psychology of the Korean People*, edited by Yoon and Choi, 92.

37. Choi and Choi, "We-ness: A Korean Discourse of Collectivism," 58.

38. Wuthnow, *"I Come Away Stronger,"* 356.

39. Ibid., 138.

40. Theresa Kelleher, "Confucianism," in *Women in World Religions*, edited by A. Sharma (Albany, NY: State University of New York Press, 1987), 138.

41. Young Ae Kim, *Han: From Brokenness to Wholeness* (Ph.D. dissertation, Claremont School of Theology, 1993), 94.

42. Ibid., 98.

43. Jean Baker Miller, *Toward a New Psychology of Women* (Boston: Beacon Press, 1976), 7–10.

44. Kyung-Hwan Min and Hai-sook Kim, "Regional Conflict in Korea: A Pathological Case of Collectivism," in *Psychology of the Korean People*, edited by Yoon and Choi, 330–49.

45. Gyuseog Han and Sug-man Choe, "Effects of Family, Region, and School Network Ties on Interpersonal Intentions and the Analysis of New Activities in Korea," in *Individualism and Collectivism*, edited by Kim et al., 213.

46. Uimyong M. Kim, "Significance of Paternalism and Communalism in the Occupational Welfare System of Korean Firms: A National Survey," in *Individualism and Collectivism*, edited by Kim et al., 252.

47. Min and Kim, "Regional Conflict in Korea," 331.

48. According to your audience, you may need to change the topic of the story to share.

Chapter 2: A Biblical Call to Communal Faith and Ministry

1. For detailed information about these practices, see Joseph D. Driskill, *Protestant Spiritual Exercises: Theology, History and Practice* (Harrisburg, PA: Morehouse Publishing, 1999).

2. This phraseology is from Charles Wesley's hymn for the 1748 opening of the New School, a Methodist endeavor in Kingwood, England. The last stanza reads: "Unite the pair so long disjoined/Knowledge and vital piety,/Learning and holiness combined,/And truth and love let all men see." See John W. Prince, *Wesley on Religious Education* (New York: The Methodist Book Concern, 1926), 122.

3. Eliezer D. Oren, "Opening Remarks," in *The Origin of Early Israel—Current Debate: Biblical, Historical and Archaeological Perspectives,* edited by Shmuel Ahituv and Elizer D. Oren (Beer-Sheva, Israel: Ben-Gurion University of the Negev Press, 1998), 2.

4. George E. Wright, *Biblical Archaeology* (Philadelphia, PA: Westminster Press, 1962), 84.

5. Albrecht Alt, *Essays on Old Testament History and Religion,* trans. R. A. Wilson (Oxford: Blackwell, 1966), 135-69.

6. Ibid., 173-237.

7. Norman Gottwald, *The Tribes of Yahweh: A Sociology of Religion of the Liberated Israel, 1250-1050 B.C.E.* (New York: Orbis Books, 1979), 191–273.

8. Jorge Pixley, "The People of God in Biblical Tradition," in *La Iglesia Popular: Between Fear and Hope. Concilium, International Journal for Theology* 6, no. 176 (1984): 17–23.

9. Thomas Thompson, "Methods and Results: A Review of Two Recent Publications," *Scandinavian Journal of the Old Testament* 15, no. 2 (2001): 306–25.

10. Israel Finkelstein, *The Archaeology of the Israelite Settlement* (Jerusalem: The Israel Exploration Society, 1988); Israel Finkelstein, "Searching for Israelite Origin," *Biblical Archaeology Review* (September/October 1988): 34–45.

11. Finkelstein says that approximately 10% of ancient Palestine's population had always been pastoral nomads who he considers ancestors of later Israel. Finkelstein, *The Archaeology of the Israelite Settlement,* 332-35.

12. Israel Finkelstein and Neil Silverman, *The Bible Unearthed: Archaeology's New Vision of Ancient Israel and the Origin of Its Sacred Texts* (New York: Free Press, 2001), 123–45; also Finkelstein, "Searching for Israelite Origin," 34.

13. Aaron Brody, Professor of Biblical Archaeology at Pacific School of Religion, on November 11, 2003.

14. Ibid.

15. Laura E. Donaldson, "Postcolonialism and Biblical Reading: An Introduction," *Semia* 75 (1996): 15–36; Jace Weaver, "From I-Hermeneutics to We-Hermeneutics: Native Americans and the Post-Colonial," *Semia* 75 (1996): 153–76.

16. Joseph Shaw, *Pilgrim People of God* (Minneapolis: Augsburg Fortress, 1990).

17. Soo-Won Lee, "The Cheong Space: A Zone of Non-exchange in Korean

Human Relationships," in *Psychology of the Korean People*, edited by Yoon and Choi, 92.

18. Shaw, *Pilgrim People of God*, 6.
19. H. Wheeler Robinson, "Hebrew Psychology," in *The People and the Book*, edited by Arthur S. Peake (Oxford: Claredon Press, 1925), 376.
20. Shaw, *Pilgrim People of God*, 5.
21. Kim, *Han*, 94.
22. Christopher J. H. Wright, *Living as the People of God: The Relevance of Old Testament Ethics* (Leicester, England: Inter-Varsity Press, 1983), 199.
23. Richard Rubenstein, "Religion and History: Power, History, and the Covenant at Sinai," in *Take Judaism, for Example: Studies toward the Comparison of Religions*, edited by Jacob Neusner (Chicago: The University of Chicago Press, 1983), 165–83; Richard Dickenson, "The People of God," *Mid-Stream, an Ecumenical Journal* 17, no. 3 (July 1978): 233–37.
24. Richard Deutsch, "The Biblical Concept of the People of God," *The South East Asia Journal of Theology* 13, no. 2 (1972): 4–13; John Willis, "Micah 2:6–8 and the 'People of God' in Micah," *Biblicalsche Zeitschrift* 14 (1970): 38–87; Seymour Siegel, "Election and the People of God—a Jewish Perspective," *The Lutheran Quarterly* 21, no. 4 (1969): 437–50.
25. Samuel W. Newell, Jr., "Many Members: The Relation of the Individual to the People of God," *Interpretation: A Journal of Bible and Theology* 5 (1951): 422.
26. Rubenstein, "Religion and History," 171.
27. Exodus 6:7; Leviticus 26:12; Deuteronomy 4:20; 26:18; 27:9; 29:12; I Samuel 7:23f; II Kings 11:17; Jeremiah 7:23; 11:4; 24:7; 30:22; 31:1; 32:38; Ezekiel 11:20; 14:11; 36:28; 37:23, 27; Zechariah 2:15; 8:8.
28. Siegel, "Election and the People of God—a Jewish Perspective," 438.
29. Ibid.
30. Shaw, *Pilgrim People of God*, 5.
31. Wright, *Living as the People of God*, 200.
32. Ibid., 198.
33. Newell, "Many Members," 416.
34. H. H. Rowley, *The Re-discovery of the Old Testament* (Philadelphia: The Westminster Press, 1946), 214.
35. Newell, "Many Members," 416–22; D. E. Hollenberg, "Nationalism and 'the Nations' in Isaiah XL–LV," *Vetus Testamentum* 19, no. 1 (January 1969): 23–36.
36. John Willis, "Exclusivistic and Incluvistic Aspects of the Concept of 'The People of God' in the Book of Isaiah," *Restoration Quarterly* 40, no. 1 (1998): 12.
37. Gerhard Lohfink, *Does God Need the Church? Towards a Theology of the People of God*, translated by Linda Maloney (Collegeville, MN: The Liturgical Press, 1999), 21.
38. Ibid., 83, 106; Juan Antonio Estrada, "People of God," in *Mysterium Liberationis: Fundamental Concepts of Liberation Theology*, edited by Ignacio Ellacuria and Jon Sobrino (New York: Orbis Books, 1993), 604–5.

39. Daniel Harrington, *New Testament Perspectives on the Church and Judaism* (Minneapolis: Fortress Press, 1980), 10.

40. Ibid., 11–12.

41. Musa Dube, *Postcolonial Feminist Interpretation of the Bible* (St. Louis: Chalice Press, 2000), 17.

42. Ibid.

Chapter 3: A Biblical Community in the New Testament

1. Dennis Jacobsen, review of *The Shalom Church: The Body of Christ as Ministering Community,* by Craig Nessan, *The Shalom Church* (Minneapolis: Fortress Press, 2010), back cover.

2. George Worgul, "People of God, Body of Christ: Pauline Ecclesiological Contrasts," *Biblical Theology Bulletin* 12, no. 1 (January 1982): 24–28.

3. Ibid., 25.

4. James Breed, "The Church as the 'Body of Christ': A Pauline Analogy," *Theological Review* 6, no. 2 (1985): 9–14.

5. Dale Martin, *The Corinthian Body* (New Haven: Yale University Press, 1995); Halvor Moxnes, "The Quest for Honor and the Unity of the Community in Romans 12 and in the Orations of Dio Chrysostom," in *Paul in His Hellenistic Context,* edited by Troels Engberg-Pedersen (Minneapolis: Fortress Press, 1994), 203–30; Gordon D. Fee, *The First Epistle to the Corinthians,* The New International Commentary on the New Testament Series (Grand Rapids: Wm. B. Eerdmans, 1987).

6. Fee, *The First Epistle to the Corinthians,* 2.

7. Martin, *The Corinthian Body,* 86.

8. Fee, *The First Epistle to the Corinthians,* 4.

9. Martin, *The Corinthian Body,* 86.

10. Ibid., 163.

11. Ibid., 21.

12. Ibid., 92–93.

13. Ibid., Chapter 3.

14. Ibid., 70. Here I rely on Dale Martin's extensive research of Corinthian conflicts, and below is a summary of his analysis.

15. Ibid., 86.

16. Ibid., 68; Fee, *The First Epistle to the Corinthians,* 612.

17. Martin, *The Corinthian Body,* 68.

18. Elisabeth Schüssler Fiorenza, *In Memory of Her: A Feminist Theological Reconstruction of Christian Origins* (New York: Crossroad, 1983), 218.

19. Fee, *The First Epistle to the Corinthians,* 601.

20. Barbara Field, "The Discourses behind the Metaphor 'The Church Is the Body of Christ' as Used by St. Paul and the 'Post-Paulines,'" *Asia Journal of Theology* 6 (April 1992): 101.

21. Breed, "The Church as the 'Body of Christ,'" 13.

22. I Corinthians 12–15.

23. Field, "The Discourses behind the Metaphor," 90.
24. Fee, *The First Epistle to the Corinthians*, 19; Field, "The Discourses behind the Metaphor," 96.
25. Elisabeth Schüssler Fiorenza criticizes that although throughout I Corinthians Paul challenges the hierarchical body ideology, he takes ambiguous positions of the male-female hierarchy. Schüssler Fiorenza, *In Memory of Her*, 248.
26. Field, "The Discourses behind the Metaphor," 96.
27. Fee, *The First Epistle to the Corinthians*, 601.
28. Ibid., 616.
29. Breed, "The Church as the 'Body of Christ,'" 14.
30. Jerome Murphy-O'Connor, *Becoming Human Together: The Pastoral Anthropology of St. Paul* (Wilmington: Michael Glazier, Inc., 1982), 175.
31. Schüssler Fiorenza, *In Memory of Her*, 218.
32. Fika van Rensburg, "The Church as the Body of Christ," in *Catholicity and Secession: A Dilemma?* edited by Paul G. Schrotenboer (Kampen, The Netherlands: J. H. Kok Publishing Company, 1992), 39.
33. Robert H. Gundry, *Soma in Biblical Theology: With Emphasis on Pauline Anthropology* (Cambridge: Cambridge University Press, 1976), 222.
34. Murphy-O'Connor, *Becoming Human Together*, 175–76.
35. van Rensburg, "The Church as the Body of Christ," 36–42.
36. Breed, "The Church as the 'Body of Christ,'" 14.
37. Murphy-O'Connor, *Becoming Human Together*, 175.
38. Yong Ting Jin, "A Protestant Perspective," in *We Dare to Dream: Doing Theology as Asian Women*, edited by Virginia Fabella and Sun Ai Lee Park (Maryknoll, NY: Orbis Books, 1989), 46.
39. Schüssler Fiorenza, *In Memory of Her*, 218; Agatha Mei-yuk Wong, "The Ministries of Women in Paul's Letter," in *Asian Women Doing Theology: Report from Singapore Conference*, November 20-29, 1987 (Hong Kong Asian Women's Resource Center for Culture and Theology [AWRC], 1989), 20–29.
40. Dube, *Postcolonial Feminist Interpretations of the Bible*, 13.
41. Ibid.
42. Leo Lieberman, *Memories of Laughter & Garlic* (Margate, NJ: Comtec Publishing, 1999), 233.

Chapter 4: A Pedagogy for Communal Faith

1. In United Methodist congregations, the Staff/Pastor-Parish Relations Committee (SPPRC) is the locally elected body that works with a bishop's cabinet to facilitate the move of clergy between local churches. A bishop appoints clergy to a congregation after consultation with a local church.
2. Joe Holland and Peter Henriot, S.J., *Social Analysis: Linking Faith and Justice* (Maryknoll, NY: Orbis Books, 1990), 8–9.
3. Ibid., 8 (emphasis added).

4. Jane Vella, *Learning to Listen, Learning to Teach: The Power of Dialogue in Educating Adults* (San Francisco: Jossey-Bass, 2002), 4.

5. Holland and Henriot, *Social Analysis*, 9.

6. Thomas H. Groome, *Christian Religious Education: Sharing Our Story and Vision* (New York: Harper and Row, 1980), 5.

7. Philosophy once was called theology's handmaiden. John Dewey effectively recast it as that of education: "If we are willing to conceive of education as the process of forming fundamental dispositions, intellectual and emotional, toward nature and fellow men, philosophy may be defined as the general theory of education. There is nothing that education is subordinate to save more education." Dewey as quoted in William F. O'Neill, *Educational Ideologies: Contemporary Expression of Educational Philosophy* (Santa Monica, CA: Goodyear Publishing, 1981), 6.

8. Donald W. Oliver, *Education and Community: A Radical Critique of Innovative Schooling* (Berkeley, CA: McCutchan Publishing Company, 1976), 46.

9. Ibid, 179.

10. Christine Eaton Blair, *The Art of Teaching the Bible: A Practical Guide for Adults* (Louisville, KY: Geneva Press, 2001), 7–23.

11. Franz Kafka, *The Trial* (New York: Schocken Books, 1957), 153.

12. Donald W. Oliver with Kathleen Waldron Gershman, *Education, Modernity, and Fractured Meaning: Toward a Process Theory of Teaching and Learning* (Albany: State University of New York Press, 1989), 14–15.

13. Ibid.

14. Ibid, 183–85.

15. This is nicely summed up in the last stanza of a hymn that Charles Wesley wrote for the 1748 opening of the New School in Kingswood, England:

    Unite the pair so long disjoined,
    Knowledge and vital piety,
    Learning and holiness combined,
    And truth and love let all men see.

    See John W. Prince, *Wesley on Religious Education* (New York: The Methodist Book Concern, 1926), 122.

16. Shel Silverstein, *Falling Up* (New York: HarperCollins, 1996), 7.

17. This exercise is adopted from a class activity that I learned in Shared Praxis for Religious Education and Pastoral Ministry course taught by Dr. Thomas Groome at Boston College during the fall semester of 1994.

18. The song was released on his 1978 album *Living Room Suite*. Lyrics are available at http://www.harrychapin.com/music/flowers.shtml.

Chapter 5: A Curriculum for Communal Faith

1. Groome, *Christian Religious Education*, 3–19.

2. Elliot W. Eisner, *The Educational Imagination: On the Design and Evaluation of School Programs*, 2nd ed. (New York: Macmillan Publishing Co., 1985), 39–40.

3. Ibid., 378. Maria Harris, in her discussion of Eisner's work, describes null curriculum this way: "This is the curriculum that exists because it does not exist; it is what is left out. But the point of including it is that ignorance or the absence of something is not neutral. It skews the balance of options we might consider, alternatives from which we might choose, or perspectives that help us see. The null curriculum includes areas left out (content, themes, points of view) and procedures left unused (the arts, play, critical analysis). See Harris, *Fashion Me a People* (Louisville, KY: Westminster/John Knox Press, 1989), 69.
4. Eisner, *The Educational Imagination*, 378.
5. Harris, *Fashion Me a People*, 63, (her italics).
6. Karen B. Tye, *Basics of Christian Education* (St. Louis, MO: Chalice Press, 2000), 32.
7. Harris, *Fashion Me a People*, 16.
8. Tye, *Basics of Christian Education*, 37–38.
9. Robert Wuthnow, *After the Baby Boomers: How Twenty- and Thirty-Somethings Are Shaping the Future of American Religion* (Princeton, NJ: Princeton University Press, 2007).
10. Ibid.
11. Thomas Beaudoin, *Virtual Faith: The Irreverent Spiritual Quest of Generation X* (San Francisco: Jossey-Bass, 2000).
12. Robert Kegan, *In Over Our Heads: The Mental Demands of Modern Life* (Cambridge, MA: Harvard University Press, 1994).
13. Ibid., 103.
14. Ibid., 104.
15. Harris, *Fashion Me a People*, 47 (her italics).

Chapter 6: Pulling It Together

1. Linda Vogel, *Religious Education of Older Adults* (Birmingham, AL: Religious Education Press, 1983).
2. Robert Kegan, *The Evolving Self: Problem and Process in Human Development* (Cambridge, MA: Harvard University Press, 1982), 114.
3. Ibid., 115.

Chapter 7: Communal Bible Study and Preaching

1. Blair, *The Art of Teaching the Bible.*
2. Kwok Pui-lan, *Discovering the Bible in the Non-biblical World* (Maryknoll, NY: Orbis Books, 1995), 30.
3. Fernando Segovia, *Decolonizing Biblical Studies: A View from the Margins* (Maryknoll, NY: Orbis Books, 2000), 119-32.
4. Finkelstein, "Searching for Israelite Origin,": 34-45; Finkelstein, *The Archaeology of the Israelite Settlement*; Finkelstein and Silverman, *The Bible Unearthed.*
5. Finkelstein, *The Archaelogy of the Israelite Settlement*, 332-335.
6. Finkelstein and Silverman, *The Bible Unearthed*, 123–45.

7. Kwok, *Discovering the Bible in the Non-biblical World*, 30.

8. For detailed interpretations of the Exodus of these different communities, please see Chapter 10.

9. Dube, *Postcolonial Feminist Interpretation of the Bible*, 17.

10. Ibid.

11. Nami Kim, "'My/Our' Comfort Not at the Expense of 'Somebody Else's': Toward a Critical Global Feminist Theology," *Journal of Feminist Studies in Religion* 21, no. 2 (2005): 75–94.

12. Dube, *Postcolonial Feminist Interpretation of the Bible*, 123.

13. Sandra Schneiders, *The Revelatory Text: Interpreting the New Testament as Sacred Scripture* (San Francisco: HarperSanFrancisco, 1991), 55-57.

14. All of the narrative parts were taken from a sermon that I preached at the Consultation for Asians/Asian North Americans in Theological Education sponsored by the Association of Theological Schools of the United States and Canada held in Redondo Beach, California, on Saturday, February 5, 2005. I present this sermon here as an example for two reasons: 1) a sermon written in a narrative form more closely embodies how I teach a Bible study class than an exegetical one; 2) I demonstrate how postcolonial biblical hermeneutics and the 5Rs model can be utilized pedagogically in preaching.

15. John Shelby Spong, *Liberating the Gospels: Reading the Bible with Jewish Eyes: Freeing Jesus from 2000 Years of Misunderstanding* (San Francisco, CA: HarperSanFrancisco, 1996), 46–53.

Chapter 8: Communal Bible Study II

1. Blair, *The Art of Teaching the Bible*, 36–40.

2. Vella, *Learning to Listen, Learning to Teach*, 3–27.

3. Blair, *The Art of Teaching the Bible*, 24–49.

4. Norma Cook Everist and Susan K. Nachtigal, "Making the Connections," in *Lifelong Learning: A Guide to Adult Education in the Church*, edited by Rebecca Grothe (Minneapolis: Augsburg Press, 1997), 169.

5. Ibid.

6. Ibid., 176.

7. Wenh-In Ng, "Three Paradigms of Reading and Interpreting the Bible," a handout distributed at a Bible Study Workshop at the Annual Meeting of PANAAWTM (Pacific, Asian, and North American Asian Women in Theology and Ministry) held in San Anselmo, California, on March 7, 2003.

8. Ng summarizes the distinct features of each interpretation as follows: 1) Traditional interpretation "spiritualizes" material issues; is heavily doctrinal; interprets the Bible from the perspective of the New Testament, especially Paul's letters; relies on the New Testament, especially Paul; is biased in favor of Christian cultures; expects ministers as sole interpreter of the text. 2) Liberal interpretation focuses on scholars' findings through scientific studies of the text; puts emphasis on the individual; tends to personalize and psychologize the meaning of the text found by scholars; is interested in generating

knowledge, feelings, and personal reactions in connections with the text; is often linked to private morality, easing burden, coping, etc. 3) Liberationist interpretation puts emphasis on community and social transformation; is guided by questions like whether newly interpreted texts bring new light on the marginalized of the society; is action-oriented in terms of connecting the text with life.

9. Leonardo Boff, *Praying with Jesus and Mary: Our Father, Hail Mary* (Maryknoll, NY: Orbis Books, 2005), 75–87.

10. Thomas Groome, *Christian Religious Education: Sharing Our Story and Vision* (San Francisco: Harper & Row, 1980), 33-55. Groome argues that Jesus preached and taught the reign of God in continuity with core convictions of his Jewish tradition, which is crystallized in the notion of Shalom, and the Lord's Prayer is one expression of that conviction. Therefore, here I borrowed Groome's interpretation of the Reign of God and Shalom to explain the meaning of the Lord's Prayer.

11. I found it interesting that both the firefighter in Everist and Nachtigal's study group and the firefighter in my Traveling Bible Study named unnecessary death due to human greed.

12. Thomas Groome, *Sharing Faith: A Comprehensive Approach to Religious Education & Pastoral Ministry* (San Francisco: HarperCollins, 1991), 146–48.

13. Ibid., 146.

14. Adopted from Everist and Nachtigal, "Making the Connections," 191.

Chapter 9: Communal Church Administration and Program Development

1. Lovett Weems, Jr., *Church Leadership: Vision, Team, Culture, and Integrity* (Nashville: Abingdon Press, 1993), 42.

2. Jackson Carroll, "Leadership and the Study of the Congregation," in *Studying Congregations: A New Handbook*, edited by Nancy Ammerman, et al. (Nashville: Abingdon Press, 1998), 180.

3. Weems, *Church Leadership*, 62–66.

4. Carroll, "Leadership and the Study of the Congregation," 170.

5. Ibid., 180–81. Also see Jackson Carroll, *As One with Authority: Reflective Leadership in Ministry* (Louisville, KY: Westminster/John Knox Press, 1991), 97–118. Carroll describes three core tasks of pastoral leadership: 1) Meaning interpretation, 2) Community formation, 3) Empowering public ministry.

6. Carroll, "Leadership and the Study of the Congregation," 181.

7. Ibid.

8. Ibid., 183–84 (his italics).

9. According to Jackson Carroll, the data collection and analysis are usually done by a special task force formed for a visioning process. It is one of the first and fundamental tasks of the group. See Carroll, "Leadership and the Study of the Congregation," 185.

10. Carroll lists group discussions such as town hall meetings under the visioning task force's responsibility. Carroll, "Leadership and the Study of the Congregation," 185.
11. Ibid., 185–86.
12. Ibid., 187.
13. Ibid.

Chapter 10: Creating an Interculturally Communal Church

1. According to Hyondok Choe, a Korean German philosopher, the concept of multiculturality describes only the factual existence of various cultures; it does not say anything about the relationship between or among these cultures. Choe, "Introduction to Intercultural Philosophy: Its Concept and History," in *Communication and Solidarity in the Era of Globalization: In Quest of Intercultural Philosophy*, edited by Department of Philosophy of Chonnam National University (Gwangju, Korea: Chonnam National University Press, 2006), 16.
2. Ibid., 5–23.
3. Ibid., 16.
4. Kathleen Turpin, "Realities, Visions and Promises of a Multicultural Future," co-authored with Mary Elizabeth Moore, Boyung Lee, Ralph Casas, Lynn Bridgers and Veronice Miles. *Religious Education* 99, no. 3 (Summer 2004): 287–315.
5. Ibid., 297.
6. Ibid., 298.
7. Ibid., 299.
8. Ibid.
9. "The Exodus: One Narrative, Many Readings," in *Voices from the Margin: Interpreting the Bible in the Third World*, edited by R. S. Sugirtharajah (Maryknoll, NY: Orbis Books, 1991).
10. Choe, "Introduction to Intercultural Philosophy," 16.
11. Dube, *Postcolonial Feminist Interpretation of the Bible*, 185.
12. Ibid., 185–86.
13. Kwok Pui-lan, *Postcolonial Imagination and Feminist Theology* (Louisville, KY: Westminster John Knox Press, 2005), 19.
14. Nami Kim, "'My/Our' Comfort Not at the Expense of 'Somebody Else's,'" 75–94.
15. Kwok, *Postcolonial Imagination and Feminist Theology*, 37.
16. Ibid., 43.
17. Ibid., 57.
18. María Pilar Aquino and Maria José Rosado-Nunes, eds., *Feminist Intercultural Theology: Latina Explorations for a Just World* (Maryknoll, NY: Orbis Books, 2007), 15.
19. Eisner, *The Educational Imagination*; Harris, *Fashion Me a People*.
20. Aquino and Rosado-Nunes, *Feminist Intercultural Theology*, 14–15.
21. Ibid., 17.

Author Index

Subject Index